1 MONTH OF
FREE
READING

at

www.ForgottenBooks.com

By purchasing this book you are eligible for one month membership to ForgottenBooks.com, giving you unlimited access to our entire collection of over 1,000,000 titles via our web site and mobile apps.

To claim your free month visit:

www.forgottenbooks.com/free758840

ISBN 978-0-484-61202-9
PIBN 10758840

TO

THE LADY NOEL BYRON,

𝕿𝖍𝖊𝖘𝖊 𝖁𝖊𝖗𝖘𝖊𝖘

ARE INSCRIBED BY

THE AUTHOR,

IN GRATEFUL ACKNOWLEDGMENT OF MANY ACTS OF
KINDNESS AND FRIENDSHIP.

All Souls' College,
June 10*th,* 1840.

DEDICATORY STANZAS

TO THE

SPIRIT OF BEAUTY.

THE beautiful, that Inner Sun
    Which quickens earth, and air, and sea,
Has held, since life her course begun,
    The Poet's heart in fee.

From spirits of immortal sway,
    Before whose dauntless eagle eyes,
Open and palpable as day,
    Her naked glory lies;

Down to the least, who hear alone
    Far echoes of her footstep fall,
We gather round her dazzling throne
    Sworn liegemen, one and all.

Queen over heaven-embracing space
    Her effluence wanders unconfined;
Each has her, in a chosen place,
    For his own worship shrined—

Whether in woods, by sunny streams,
    At nature's side she rest apart,
Or clothe her presence with the dreams
    Of consecrating art.

Or tired of dead unchanging things,
    She seek what only soul can give,
Shed softly, as on Angel wings,
    From looks that move and live;

Her sacred shadow veil'd, and dim
To eyes profane, and leave untold
Her chosen Home for him:

To this one fealty confined,
That firm in faith, and loyal love, he bring
To BEAUTY—by the heart enshrined—
His vassal offering.

LADY AGNES.

It is the hour, when through the air
    The Elves of silence creep,
And maidens, with unbraided hair,
    Sink into blooming sleep.

The Lady Agnes, lightly lifting
    Her dove-like hazel eyes,
From room to room, like sunlight shifting,
    To her calm chamber hies.

Beautiful Agnes! as she went
   By stair and gallery wall,
There seemed a mellowing glory lent
   Unto that wild old hall.

Even portraits, grim with iron thought,
   And monsters of the loom,
Were softened, as if near her, nought
   Could keep its natural gloom.

But as her youthful beauty stole
   Through the long corridor,
There spread a passion on her soul,
   Shadowing its brightness o'er.

Her eye, among the imaged dead
   No face of love could see—
" Alas for her who died," she said,
   " In giving life to me.

" These warrior portraits stern and old,
　" Make sad this echoing place ;
" It would have soothed me to behold
　My mother's angel face.

" But she was taken suddenly
　From human hope and fear,
And lives but in the memory
　Of those who loved her here.

" But I, who never saw her—I
　Question and question still ;
Had her dear likeness smiled on high,
　I might have gazed my fill.

" Dreaming that life within the eye,
　Was kindling more and more,
I could have sat for ever by
　Her shadow on the floor.

" And if my spirit lacking strength
    Felt desolate and sad,
I could have watched her, till at length
    Her looks had made me glad.

" Oh tell me, tell me, Nurse, to night,
    Was she not mild and fair?
Which were the rooms of her delight,
    What garments did she wear?"

" Your mother, sweet," the Nurse replies,
    " Indeed was wondrous fair ;
Like yours her dove-like hazel eyes,
    Like yours her auburn hair.

" In that same room, she loved the best,
    You sleep, my child, each night ;
And like an angel, she was drest,
    Ever in raiment white.

" But these are stories for the day,
　When summer sunbeams fall
With searching and enlivening ray
　Around this wild old hall.

" Suffer not now, such thoughts of pain
　About your heart to stay,
Or the dim workings of the brain
　Will chase all sleep away."

Still feeling on her orphaned breast
　A weight of tender gloom,
She reached the chamber of her rest,
　Her mother's favourite room ;

And sinking with a quiet sigh
　Into the offered chair,
She scarcely felt the nurse untie
　Her waving auburn hair.

Within that consecrated space,
   You could not but have felt,
Touched by the spirit of the place,
   That THERE a Virgin dwelt.

There seemed a presence half divine
   Floating unseen above—
The shadow of calm thoughts, the sign
   Of maiden faith, and love;

As if her spotless heart had shed
   A dew of pureness there,
Which brooded o'er the placid bed,
   And glorified the air.

Beautiful Agnes! sitting still
   Before a mirror tall,
Letting the auburn curls at will
   On her white shoulder fall.

LADY AGNES.

She gazed into the solemn skies,
   Now hung with boundless night;
Her large uplifted hazel eyes
   Floating in liquid light;

Whilst from her fresh and lucent skin,
   A lustre seemed to pour,
Like delicate pink tints, within
   Shells from an Indian shore.

In pensive silence thus the maid
   Her loveliness undrest;
The nurse in silence gave her aid,

Beautiful Agnes ! may she sleep
   Until the golden day,
Beneath an angel's wing, to keep
   All evil things away.

But soft—she wakes, as if in fear ;
   What sights or sounds invade
The wavering eye—or dreaming ear,
   To make her thus afraid ?

The nurse was summoned to her side.
   " Is then my darling ill?"
" No, but the lamp, dear nurse," she cried ;
   " You left it burning still."

" Nay, look, my love, no lamp is near,
   The room was black as night;
This taper I have carried here—
   There is no other light."

" Have I then roused you up in vain?
   I must have dreamt," she said;
And on the silken couch again
   Down dropped her flower-like head.

But on the closing of the door,
   Again the room was bright;
O'er cornice, curtain, ceiling, floor,
   Fluttered that wondrous light.

High o'er her pillow, she beheld
   A glory gliding nigher,
From which, as from a fountain, welled
   Floods of innocuous fire ;

And in the middle of the light
   A wingèd woman there,
With hazel eyes, and raiment white,
   And waving auburn hair.

Upon the silent girl below,
    Her looks of beauty fell,
Speaking of peace earth cannot know,
    And love ineffable.

And Agnes gazed a little while,
    Then prayed for strength and grace,
Till both came issuing from the smile
    Upon that woman's face.

Whether in words, to human sense,
    The spirit found its way,
Or by some mystic influence,
    The maiden could not say.

But words, or thoughts, an angel sway
    Lived on her heart like balm,
So that her senses, as she lay,
    Were steeped in wondrous calm.

And thus, a heaven-sent messenger,
Upon her human child,
Scarcely more beautiful than her,
The spirit mother smiled.

Mother and daughter felt through death,
Their hearts grow one in love;
Delicious human tears beneath,
And seraph smiles above.

And then the Aspect told the maid,
By word, or look, or sign,
That she must pass from earthly shade
Into a light divine;

That it had pleased the Lord, to give
Them both a precious boon,
And that her child should come to live
With her to-morrow noon.

When this was said, the air grew dim,
    And Agnes felt her brain
Down a bright stream of vision swim,
    To slumbrous depths again.

Oh! there was trouble in the hall
    When Agnes told her tale,
A shadow of strange fear on all—
    She only did not quail.

She only said, " This wondrous show,
    Though true and clear it seem,
By my own reason taught, I know,
    May only be a dream.

" And if a dream it be, why soon
    The cloud it leaves is gone;
But if a spirit—then at noon,
    God's holy will be done."

But nothing they could find, to show
   One trace of feverish heat;
As soft and calm as falling snow,
   Her maiden pulses beat.

" Cool is her blood," they said; " unriven
   The peaceful nerves and brain;
Our skill is idle—and with Heaven
   The issue must remain.

" Let her go forth to usual things,
   The tasks of every day,
Until this dream, which round her clings,
   Dies silently away.

Pensively then the maiden's eye
　　Turned to the climbing sun;
But ever, as the hour went by,
　　Its usual task was done,

Until that sun had ceased to climb
　　The fathomless mid-heaven,
And noon was drawing near, the time
　　To holy music given.

Her minstrel did not come; and tired
　　With waiting on so long,
She sat her down, like one inspired,
　　And poured her soul in song.

" Christe, miserere mei,
　　Præbe, Mater, lucem,
Miserere, Agne Dei,
　　Per æternum crucem."

The Minstrel stealing in alone,
   Stood tranced beside the door;
"For sounds came forth," he said, "unkno
   Except in Heaven, before."

And often he was wont to say,
   And to his faith did cling,
That those, who listened on that day,
   Had heard an angel sing.

At once the song stops hurriedly,
   As if without her will;
Though floods of viewless melody
   Seem eddying round her still.

Gracefully then the maiden bent
   Over her throbbing lute,
As if to sweep the strings she meant;
   But still those strings were mute.

The dial points to noon—and hark!
    The old clock shakes its tower;
Yet, strange to say, she did not mark
    The coming of that hour.

A sunbeam touched her placid brow,
    If earthly beam it were,
And tinted with a golden glow
    Her trembling auburn hair.

She stirred not—and it seemed to lie
    A glory on her head;
But when that splendour had passed by,
    They found—that she was dead!

So gentle was her death—so blest—
    Under the covering cross,
That even those who loved her best,
    Could scarcely mourn their loss.

They laid her, Heaven's selected bride,
    Her mother's grave within—
Two sainted sleepers, side by side,
    Far from the strife of sin.

Beautiful Agnes!—may she sleep
    Thus, till the judgment day,
Beneath an angel's wing, to keep
    All evil things away.

RESEMBLANCE.

LINES SUGGÈSTED BY A REMARKABLE LIKENESS
BETWEEN TWO YOUNG LADIES.

WHAT solemn law, what changeless end,
    The shaping hand of Nature guides,
So that with outward form may blend,
    The spirit that within resides?

And how that spirit working on,
    Frames for itself a fitting shrine,
And what the purport, stamped upon
    Each varying motion, look, and line?

To us are unrevealèd things,
  Far hidden in the clouds, which lower
Above the dark unsounded springs
  Of motive will, and living power.

But though we cannot always guess
  The scope of her unswerving plan,
Nature is never meaningless,
  Nor sway'd by blind caprice, like man:

Not idly then of late, she drew
  Forth from her ever-sounding loom,
Those living robes she wove for you,
  Twin beauty, and resembling bloom:

Though slight the tie, if human thought
  Measure this mystic union well,
Its inner essence *may* be fraught
  With deeper powers than thought can tell.

Perchance, it mutely prophesies
　　Of the To-come, whilst yet afar,
Of Ante-natal destinies
　　Launched from the same impending star.

Perchance, apportioned as his own,
　　One Angel watches both bright flowers;
Perchance, from his refulgent throne
　　Upon each maiden brow, in hours

Of peril, troubled fear, and need,
　　The shadow of one love is thrown;
And in your spotless hearts, the seed
　　Of the same calming amaranth sown.

So that, when o'er this desert dim

Believe at least, that it was wise
　　Your graceful reverence to shew
For all the unknown deep, that lies
　　About our path, where'er we go.

That interchange of happy laughter,
　　Of emblem blooms, and gentle speech,
Should be a well-spring, ever after,
　　Of pleasant kindliness, to each.

The symbol flowers you gave, must die;
　　May what they shadowed forth, live still;
Let not one drop of love run by,
　　Which Time's wild river brings at will.

CIRCASSIAN WAR SONG.

———

THOUGH Russia, cheating, crushing, yet
    Her web of ruin twines,
Along Caucasian hills, unset
    The star of Freedom shines.

The Czar upon his marshy plains,
    May count and drill his men;
More must be done, before he gains
    The mountain lion's den.

War is to him a science cold
    Of numbers and array—
Enough of lead, enough of gold,
    Enough of food and pay;

As if men's hearts that sink and swell,
    Like wooden chessmen were;
As if the strength of central hell
    Could shake a brave despair.

We'll teach this monarch of machines,
    What living souls can do,
When noble ends, and noble means,
    Conspire to bring them through.

Yes! when blood-red the firing glares
    Through floods of smoke, and thunder,
When every ravening echo, tears
    The trembling crags in sunder;

When warlike pomp of fife and drum,
   And columns clustering deep,
Mere rottenness and dust become,
   Against God's mountain-steep ;

The planning, marching, numbering Czar,
   Among his tools, may find
That something else is strong in war,—
   The Spirit of mankind.

THE POETASTER'S PLEA.

A FAMILIAR EPISTLE TO W. E. GLADSTONE, ESQ., M. P.

ONE, of a long-oppressed insulted crew,
At length, dear Gladstone, I appeal to you;
I do not mean the warrior of the state,
Clothed in bright armour at the temple's gate :
Set in the front of battle, to uphold
The truth that streams in glory from of old;
To praise thy bearing in that arduous fight,
Proud friends, and unresentful foes unite;
And the hushed spirits of the future see
Even now, a lord of human kind in thee.
Not to the man or statesman, now I speak ;
Another, who is yet the same, I seek,—
One of a joyous company, who hied
Through the green fields along the river side,
Those laughing fields, which wear for you and me
A garment of perpetual youth and glee,

Where voices call us, that are heard no more,
And our "lost Pleiad" brightens as before.

To one I turn—the monarch of debate,
President Minos of our little state,
Who, when we met to give the world the law
About Confucius, Cæsar, or Jack Straw,
Saw with grave face the unremitting flow
Of puffs and jellies from the shop below ;
At the right moment, called us to forsake
Intrusive fruit, and unattending cake ;
And if unheeded, on the stroke of four,
With rigid hand closed the still-opening door,
Denouncing ever after in a trice,
That heinous breach of privilege—an ice—
To one, who in his editorial den
Clenched grimly an eradicating pen,
Confronting frantic poets with calm eye,
And dooming hardened metaphors to die.
Who, if he found his young adherents fail,
The ode unfinished. uncommenced the tale.

With the next number bawling to be fed,

And its false feeders latitant or fled,

Sat down unflinchingly to write it all,

And kept the staggering project from a fall.

Nor men, nor gods, nor yet the trade, alas!

Will license middling poetry to pass;

So Horace tells us, but is Horace right?

I own I think his dictum merely spite.

The pampered favourite only means to say

That Roman Grub-streets bored his soul away,

Ecstatic bards beset his path in swarms,

And Bavius clasped him in fraternal arms.

Hoarse Mœvius talked his best to make him stare,

Whilst he sat shuddering in his elbow chair;

Hence, full of bile, he raised his arm on high,

And smote that hapless legion, hip and thigh.

Succeeding times have echoed on the strain,

And spent their fury on the tribe in vain.

In self-conceit invulnerably mailed,

We stand, however savagely assailed,

THE POETASTER'S PLEA.

pour into the drowsy ear of time

ever ebbing tides of blank and rhyme.

mbs there are, no doubt, by scribbling made,

of a shapeless star—for every shade

iny-coloured life alike unfit—

deem themselves the miracles of wit.

igh all the forms of our great art they crawl,

icing nothing, but infesting all.

some mysterious wisdom make pretence,

at plain strength of head, and stalwart sense;

ver then that rhyme is not a knife,

en at their will, the oyster—life;

sour and bitter, and fermenting fast

nto eager vinegar at last,

ie vexed world wraps, in one general curse,

luckless vagabond who writes a verse.

etting these aside, a whining few,

loose your dogs against our harmless crew?

y own cost I give the world my own—

is not please you? leave it then alone.

To the dull page no law chains down your eye;

No act of parliament compels to buy ;

No general warrant do I hold, to keep

Members from their diurnal prose and sleep,

Squires from the Derby, lawyers from the courts,

Or you, from those seducing blue reports,

Where Elliot does his best stale fish to cry,

And Lin to blacken the Barbarian Eye.

What, though a thousand holders of the quill

Can write as well, or better if you will?

What, though I never hope to see my rhyme

Surmount one ripple of the stream of time?

Why should I stay my hand? or blot what lends

A touch of pleasure to some partial friends?

Whilst praise and fame, in every grade belong

Unto the sister arts—design and song.

Freely we grant our talents are but small,

But is it better to have none at all?

Unridiculed by men or Gods, we see

A sketcher, sitting under every tree.

Not theirs the hands, that can express at will,
Gigantic visions with unerring skill.
No mighty genius moulds the vast design,
No labouring thought inheres in every line;
Near the rapt eye, as still the shapes they trace,
There floats no mild unfathomable face,
Whose human beauty melts into seraphic grace.
Still, praised themselves, they teach us to admire
The depth which awes, the models that inspire:
Were there none such (like gradual hills set high
To parley with the peaks that drink the sky,)
Apelles might have lived and died unknown,
And Phidias left unscraped the Parian stone.
So, but for us, a scorned, a trampled throng,
Homage would fail the sacred kings of song;
Did not our spirits catch the dawning blaze,
Reflect the glory, and transmit the rays,
Beams of the sun without an atmosphere,
Great poets would be useless aliens here.
If still you shake your head, I can but say,

That thus I smoothe the roughness of the way.

At Eton taught to bear, and to forbear,

I boast of no magnificent despair ;

I am not good, or bad enough, to know

The isolation of especial woe ;

Still there are times, when fever and unrest

Besiege the silent fortress of the breast;

Unspoken heaviness and cares unshown,

Which yet are bitter to endure alone ;

When on some sunny dream cloud-shadows fall,

Or sorrows come to me that come to all—

Days of uprooted hope—of fading flowers—

Of rainbows, waning into wintry showers—

When hidden languor follows secret strife,

And the heart sickens at the length of life—

These are the seasons, which of right belong

To thoughts, which rush and kindle into song.

No idle dream of fame, no servile fear

Of the world's scorn, beset and goad me here.

Instinctively, my shattered spirits come

To look for eace within their natural home

In that small circle still, defying fate,

I can at least, or well or ill, create,

Till genial art has charmed away the pain,

And the soul strengthens to her work again.

The humblest thus appear to draw more nigh

To the great heirs of immortality—

Milton rose up, when fate grew hard to bear,

From earth to Heaven, and drew empyrean air.

From the salt bread he loathed, and paths of pa

Up alien stairs, when life was on the wane,

The Tuscan sought his seraph love again.

And Tasso kept in gloom, when hope was dead,

One brightness, from the laurel on his head.

Auguster grief was theirs, whose awful sound,

Sea-like, is heard the listening earth around—

But yet the same perennial fountains fill

The ocean-deeps, and shallows of the rill.

Though vast the space between us, not the less

We seek a common solace in distress.

Enough of this—and kindly take from me

These fragments as a poetaster's plea.

THE NIGHT AND THE DAY.

THEY met in the hour of the dim twilight,
The hour, that is neither day, nor night;
Like two proud queens, they met on high,
In that neutral space of the summer sky,
Where the evening star, when the day is done,
Shines through the haze of the sunken sun.

  The first was darkly pale—with eyes
  Deeper than are the midnight skies,
  Pale, as an Indian monarch's bride,
  The burning pyre beside;
  Yet lovely, as the seraphim,
  When pitying tears their splendour dim,

Tears shed in heaven itself, to see

The depth of human misery:

Her voice was musical, and low;

With something in its tone

Of charmèd power, that seemed to flow

From worlds to man unknown.

Beneath her broad imperial brow,

Those deep eyes darkly shone,

Pure, as the wreathèd stars below,

That glowed within her burning zone.

The second, was a brighter maiden,

Her brow with curls of gold was laden;

Her smile was sparkling, clear and free,

Though stately as a queen was she.

Her jewelled neck, and arms, were bare,

Snow-white, beneath her sunny hair—

Each vein was filled with fire, and lent

Her eye ethereal merriment;

Upon her cheek there lived a blush,

Warm, as the sunset's tender flush;

A tone in her glad voice had she,
At which, the heart beat like the sea,
When the west wind bloweth warm and free,
And a merry glance, like the smile of spring,
Which made each pulse a living thing.
But her dark rival stood, sedate,
With soothing eyes compassionate,
Whose light my very heart did fill
With visions that subdued the will,
And bowed me with a sudden sense
Of unresisted reverence;
For, by the brow divinely fraught
With incommunicable thought—
By those low tones, which seemed to be

The mighty mysteries that sleep,

In that still spirit hidden deep.

Then, as the blue-eyed maiden bent

Above her charmèd instrument,

And breathed unto the listening air,

Strains sweet enough to lull despair,

Those eyes of beauty did express

A pure and pitying tenderness,

And on her lip, there gleamed the while

A calm and melancholy smile.

THE DAY.

I am the queen of earth and sea,

Who shall dispute the palm with me?

I am lovely as of yore,

When, upon the clouded shore

Of an abysmal sea, I stood,

Enkindled by the breath of God.

All things then, that hate the light—

All the gloomy brood of night,

Fled before me, as I blest

The raging deep with peace, and rest.

Then—the proud giant of the sun,

Leapt forth his glorions race to run,

And the breathing world her course begun :

How beautiful it was, to see

Beneath *my* beams, all things that be

Awake in primal revelry ;

Oh turn to me, from the dark dull night,

For my voice is the voice of life, and light.

THE NIGHT.

Mine is the sceptre of the sky,

And mine the starry worlds on high :

Those fountains of eternal light,

Which feed the immeasurable void

With life and splendour undestroyed,

And tell that God is infinite.

Thou knowest how the midnight sky,

Fills the weak heart with purity ;

How all the dreams of wrath and sin,

That lurk the soul's lone caves within,

To make its peace their prey—take flight

Before the blessed breath of night.

Thou know'st the reverential sense

   Of God and his omnipotence;

The tears of pleasantness that rise

" Up from the heart into the eyes "—

Thou know'st the sweet and solemn fear,

As if the holy dead were near,

And the deep touch of earthly love,

When the stars are shining bright above,

And all things that about us lie

Inhale *their* immortality.

   If these have charms to move thee,

   Follow and love me.

THE DAY.

Bring all the flowers beneath the sun,

That shut their leaves when the light is gone—

For mine is the breath of the crimson rose,

Mine is every bud that blows;

O turn from the dark dull night to me,

For mine is the beauty of earth and sea—

Thy spirit shall be clear as day,

Thy smile shall be the morning ray,

Whose light, wherever it may fall,

Sheds love and blessedness o'er all.

Thy soul shall feel the soft caress

Of unimagined happiness;

For all the roses that combine

To veil the ills of life, are mine

Mine are the crowded cities, where

Mirth is always on the air—

Where no shadow can eclipse

The smile that lives upon the lips,

But all things ever seem to be

Steeped in sunny revelry.

Mine is the joyous wine-cup, bright

And burning with imprisoned light;

Mine are the melodies which fill

The heart with a voluptuous thrill,

Which cloud the spirit with excess

Of most tumultuous happiness,

And drown all sense of pain in man,

As fully as the wine cup can.

Mine are the maidens of sunny hair,

    And eyes divinely blue;

Mine is the love that knows no care,

    But yet is warm and true.

O turn to me, from the gloomy night,

For my voice is the voice of life, and light.

THE NIGHT.

Many a cycle has there been,

With gulphs of nothingness between;

Many a time have life and birth

Revisited the agèd earth:

Learn, mortal, that to me alone,

The secret things of the past are known;

THE NIGHT AND THE DAY.

Mine is every charmèd rhyme,

Freighted with spells of ancient time,

Strains divinely sweet, which sing

The deeds of many a giant king,

Whose life was mighty in each limb,

Whose soul was as the seraphim ;

I can place before thine eye

The mirror of eternity,

I can show thee imaged there

Shadows of all things that were,

And bid oblivion's self unfold

The treasures of his cavern old ;

Stately cities ever bright

With porphyry, and chrysolite ;

THE NIGHT AND THE DAY.

Mine is Babylon the great,

Mine her river desolate,

And that sky-cleaving citadel,

Above the golden halls of Bel:

Mine are the towers along the Nile

Where Power and Wisdom dwelt erewhile—

The labyrinths, whose courts enfold

The melancholy gods of old—

The obelisks, unfallen still,

On some lone Abyssinian hill,

Covered with uncouth shapes, which brood

Above the lion-haunted wood.

Hers is this world of life and breath,

But *mine* the treasuries of death;

All things holy and divine

Whose light on earth has ceased to shine,

High hopes and visions that are fled,

Pure feelings that have perishèd—

Deep love whose passionate caress

Grew still more tender in distress—

And all the genius of the dead

Which never can be rivallèd.

Mine is the music pure and deep,

Such as poets hear in sleep,

Where genius, clear as heaven above,

And quickened by intensest love,

Dreams of the beautiful and true,

Such as the cold world never knew,

And feeling soft as morning dew,

Unite, like streams upon the lea,

Into one simple melody :

Mine are the maidens who delight

With tender loveliness, like night,

With voices of a thrilling sound

Which sheddeth peace and love around,

And pensive feelings deep, that shine

Through spiritual eyes divine ;

 If these have charms to move thee,

 Follow and love me.

I covet not the incense blind,

The mad allegiance of mankind—

How should I, being the ancient queen

Of all beyond this narrow scene!

My kingdom knows nor time nor place,

It is the lone abyss of space—

The illimitable darkness thrown

Round petty systems, like a zone;

Still, though above the touch of woe,

I pity those who weep below.

As I sit, crowned with power, alone

Upon my everlasting throne,

I feel that the gloom around is rife

With the spirit of enduring life,

And cherish amid darkness dull

The image of the beautiful.

A thousand times has the light of Day

Startled those holy dreams away;

A thousand times has the brute mass

Felt God's eternal pinions pass

Through the gross element, that holds

Pale Chaos in her cumbrous folds;

I have seen it waken every time,

To be the theatre of crime.

I have seen sick dreams of unreal good,

As life and happiness pursued,

And the blessed hopes that cannot die

Again and again passed idly by.

I am wearied out at length to see

The same vain toil repeatedly—

The self-deceit, the ceaseless strife,

The utter vanity of life.

Her promised joys will end once more,

In gloom and sorrow, as of yore.

I am *very* weary of the past,

O take the peace I bring at last.

She ceased to speak, but my charmèd soul

Bowed down before her soft control;

And I left the Day with her flaunting light,

To follow the calm and starry Night.

A STARLIGHT NIGHT.

THE thin white clouds serenely move
   Athwart the blue ethereal dome ;
The silent stars are bright above,
   Each in his own eternal home,
Filling the solemn void of night,
With effluence of primal light.

Ye silent stars ! I feel that nought,
   Or heart, or world, alone can be,
And know, by human feeling taught,
   That over all yon trackless sea,
The myriad worlds that round me shi
Are linked in sympathy to mine.

Alas! each clear unsullied star
   Is but another earth like this;
The same wild hopes, and feelings *are*
   Throughout the infinite abyss:
The same vain thirst to love and know,
And all the mystery of woe.

Yet though strange grief within be folded,
   The rays we see are pure and still:
Their orbs to shine on us were moulded
   By the great Spirit's plastic will;
And this dark spot, which we contemn,
Lives in eternal light for them.

Though vexed within by countless woes,
   They sink not underneath the wound:
By means, which God on all bestows,
   The solace of their grief is found.
Leaning, like seraphs, from above,
They fill the skies with light and love.

To those who feel, the power is given
　This sign of mystery to scan,
And draw down from the stars of heaven,
　A lesson for the heart of man,
That it should cherish, in all grief,
Its own affections, as relief.

By works of love the soul must be
　To its own happiness refined;
And thus invincible and free,
　Weave ever round the subject mind
(Though gloomy as the wings of night)
An atmosphere of holy light.

TO ———

————

THERE is a magic in thy smile,
   I shall not feel again,
Which melts into my heart the while,
   Like music's mournful strain :

Though light and gay that smile may be
   As the sunbeam on the waters,
Its power is deeper upon me
   Than the smile of beauty's daughters.

Like some young flower, thou blossomest,
   Without a fear on earth;
Deep feelings, iñ thy tranquil breast,
   Are blent with graceful mirth:

Belovèd one, thou standest now,
   In our dim vale of years,
Just where the streams of childhood flow
   Into Life's sea of tears.

I know not, and I would not know,
   What Fate prepares for thee;
I know not, whether joy or woe
   Will change the soul I see.

The cherished rose may droop and die,
   Or beam in beauty's brightness;
But its deepest blush can never vie
   With the rosebud's maiden whiteness.

I SAW HER LAST.

Elle étoit de ce monde où les plus belles choses
    Ont le pire destin,
Elle veçut, ce que Vivent les roses,
    L'espace d'un matin.

I SAW her last, when love's warm light
    Lay deep within her modest eye,
When all futurity was bright
    Before her, like a summer sky—
It quieted both païn and fear,
    To see a thing so happy, near.

E 2

Yet was this blessedness, a flower
   Too delicate for earth—alas!
Its leaves were withered in an hour;
   As sunshine glideth from the grass,
And melts invisibly away,
So did she vanish from the day.

Then came soft sorrow upon all,
   That one so full of gentle grace
Beneath so rude a touch should fall;
   By eyes, that never saw her face,
Tears from the inmost heart were shed,
And all the happy mourned the dead:

They mourned her as the beautiful,
   Even as we mourn the rose's doom,
When every crimson leaf grows dull,
   And death feeds on the damask bloom;
They mourned her as she was—but I
Looked to our vanished infancy—

To those deep memories, which seem

The very fountains of the stream.

The early unforgotten things

To which the spirit ever clings,

And feels, throughout all change, to be

The seal of her identity.

With the same blood our veins were rife,

The selfsame summer gave us life,

And this was as a silken tie

Of fellowship and sympathy—

Therefore, through childhood's sunny weather,

We were, as loving twins, together;

Together in the greenwood shade,

Day after day we laughed and played;

Together, with hushed breath, drew nigh

To snare the crimson butterfly,

Or stopped to hear the throstle sing

Beneath the mellow evening.

Alas! how vain the hope I cherished,

That though the childish joys had perished,

The memory of these pleasant things
Would lend the weary spirit wings,
To flee away from care and sadness,
    From life's great sea of tossing foam,
From manhood's grief, and manhood's gladness,
    Back to her youthful home.
Alas! that sunny place is not,
A cloud has deepened o'er the spot,
So that whene'er I summon back
The faded hues of childhood's track,
There comes upon me a distress,
A sense of solemn loneliness,
Which makes my spirit for a time
Shrink from that bright and blessèd clime,
To find a home in future things,
For the deep heart's imaginings;
Since she, who shared the past with me,
    Has put on immortality.

HEATHEN LIFE.

μὴ φῦναι τὸν ἄπαντα νι-
κᾷ λόγον· τὸ δ’, ἐπεὶ φανῇ
βῆναι κεῖθεν, ὅθεν περ ἥ-
κει, πολὺ δεύτερον, ὡς τάχιστα.

SOPHOCLES.

The graceful flower expireth,

　　The shapeless rocks yet lower,

Nor storm, nor earthquake, tireth

　　The ocean's hungry roar.

The lute of softness, weareth

　　Beneath a hand of snow,

The sword of sternness, beareth

　　The battle's iron blow :

Like the fleet mirage, flieth

　　All that is soft and gay;

Gloom brightness underlieth,

　　And passeth not away.

COUNT OTTO.

Count Otto for once foregoes the chase;

Unhoped-for gladness is in his face,

For an heiress is born to his ancient race.

And Time flew by on swifter wing,

Where she grew like a flower, in the silence of spring,

With an old oak overshadowing.

Lovely in feature, and heart, and limb,
For years she clung in love to him,
Like a graceful plume round a helmet grim.

But again he neglects the reveillè horn;
He talked with the Abbot all night till morn,
Whose eyes were bright with joyful scorn.

And that fair girl, adored by all,
The life of masque and festival,
Why is she absent from the hall?

Cold, pale, and silent, in her bower,
Without a sob, from hour to hour
She sits and weeps—to smile no more—

Count Otto is idle to-day again,
His stalwart hand forgets the rein,
And tears on his cheek have left a stain:

Alas! for the fall of that ancient line!
Alas, Count Otto, for thee and thine!
Alas for *him* in Palestine.

Behind the inexorable veil,
As hope and sense and motion fail,
Totters and falls that maiden pale.

Before the impenetrable railing,
The aged sire kneels bewailing,
But all things *now* are unavailing—

Hark! hear ye not the distant swell,
The deep and melancholy knell,
Flung from the convent's iron bell?

Hark! to the masses chanted slowly,
Hark! to the blessing murmur'd lowly,
" Peace to the slumbers of the holy."

God's love can now alone restore

The heart of him, who goes no more

To rouse the stag, or track the boar.

With settled sorrow in his face,

He sits, and broods in some dark place,

The last of all that ancient race.

THE COMET.

This poem was suggested by the vague apprehensions of injury to the earth from the Comet of 1832, which were talked over, at least, if not partially acquiesced in, by a great number of persons.

WE spake of ether—of the midnight heavens,

Of the wide sea, alike in every change

The vassal of the cold and distant Moon;

Of all the solemn workings of the stars

Through her appointed cycles—of the fate

Of ruined planets—of the mystic star

In Cassiopeia, which was seen of old

By the pale shepherdess, and lated hind,

Through many a summer evening to burn,

With an intense effulgence of white light,

Which deepened into red, and then became

Darkness, in its own fury self-consumed:

Thus dropping by a gradual discourse

To Earth, and that fierce shape of erring fire

Which even then (so to the untaught mind

Imagination had interpreted

The simple fact, that in its course a Comet

Would cross the pathway sacred to the earth,)

Was winding its interminable way

Through the black infinite, a wondrous orb

Made heavy with the freight of death, and charged

To crush the earth to chaos, as a hill,

Torn from its strong foundations, in its fall

Crushes the careless traveller beneath—

To say to the wild sea, " Enough, be still,

Thy tides are numbered in Eternity ;"

To shake the rocks and mountains into dust,

Or scatter their huge limbs upon the air

Like drops of summer dew; from Caucasus,

And the ice-crowned Himala, unsurpassed

In loftiness, above Cathaian plains,

To the great mountains of the western world,

Clothed in enduring snow, or bright within

With caves of wondrous flame, and galleries,

Where the chained earthquake slumbers, light as day—

Yea, bearing earthwards on its awful car

Than this material ruin of a world

A deeper desolation, since at once

The orb of its destroying wrath must quell

All beatings of the wondrous human heart,

Must quench the sacred light of earthly love,

And wrap in death the soaring mind of man

In the sole world we know.

                What marvel then

That when my limbs were laid in pleasant sleep
My brain was haunted with dim phantasies?
That voices of strange music touched mine ear,
And said to me, A vision to thy soul
Shall prophesy, a dream upon thine eye
Shall paint the coming hour?

                            With fiery speed
I felt myself borne upward far away,
Sustained upon the unessential gloom
Of the starred empyrean, whilst around,
The azure chasms of infinity,
Yawned without limit, and unfathomable!
Then saw I all the congregated worlds
Flowing around their central suns in joy
And exultation, full of perfect life:
Most wonderful! and my delighted spirit
Drank thirstily the noble harmonies
Flung from them as they passed in glorious state.
But as I gazed in passive wonderment
Upon that radiant fleet of breathing worlds

Planets, and satellites, and wandering flames,

And the blind progress of chaotic stars

Ripening from vaporous films, until they shine

As orbèd suns of undecaying fire;

The spirit who accompanied my flight

Spoke to me once again—" I brought thee here

From the low earth up to the sacred heavens

To spare thy human nature, when the hour

Of the annihilation shall arrive;

It were not good to render visible

The divine features of thy mother earth

Made hideous in her fearful agony.

No eye of human mould could look upon

The very lineaments of desolation;

No human ear could listen to a world

Breathing forth strange unprecedented sounds

In solemn woe, or bear the single shriek

Of mighty cities startled out of sleep

Into the arms of death.—Thou shalt behold

The hour of fate prefigured—thou shalt see

God's vengeance on the dark idolatries

Of a near globe that worships the dull earth;

And hear a mighty death-dirge, from above,

Sung by the stars in their eternal course,

Unto the wide ear of the universe;

But this is not our goal; away with me."

I felt my brain grow dizzy with the speed

Of sudden flight, and when again the mist

Fled from my eyesight, in a plain I stood,

A wide green meadow on a river's brink.

A stately city with its thousand towers,

A wilderness of palaces and domes,

Bounded the southern aspect; on the north

Wild mountains of immeasurable height

Shot up into the sky—upon their sides

Undying snow dazzled the gazer's eye:

But their dread summits were unknown and dark;

The very atmosphere of life and light

The barren crags rose on—around them ever

Eternal blackness clung, Eternal calm.

I gazed around in blank astonishment;

The hills were thick with trees, but, as it seemed,

Their vegetation was not of the earth;

Upon the shapely stems, upon the leaves,

Upon the flowers beneath my feet, the seal

Of a mysterious difference was set:

All things, though not discordant, were unlike

Their kindred here—over its pebbly bed

The river murmured with an alien sound;

The winds breathed out a low peculiar tone

As they flew by; the clouds wore not the hues

Of earth; the sky was bright with other stars:

In lieu of the cold moon which rules our night,

Full in the centre of the living heavens

An orb of beauty shone majestical;

Smiling upon us with a disk as broad

As that, wherewith the mighty sun looks down,

Upon the fevered plains of Mercury

In middle summer, yet with light as mild

As the pale glow-worm in a flowery dell :

It filled the air with silver, as a lamp

Girt round with glistering spar of caverns old,

Low in the central earth : how beautiful !

How more than beautiful that smile divine

Fell on the snow-clad rocks, and silent stream !

Long gazed I there forgetful of all else,

In blissful musings wrapt; When suddenly

Once more I heard the voice angelical

Low breathing its mysterious melody

Upon the trancèd air—till the clear heavens

Were satiated with delightful sound

Beneath that queenly moon, whose glorious orb

Blent the full powers of an unclouded sun

With all the weird solemnity of night.

" This region," thus it spake to me, " is part

Of that fair planet which the sons of men

Have called their moon—and that etherial light,

That brighter Cynthia, upon which thine eyes

Are fixed with such deep love, does not thy heart,

Thy human heart, taught by some magic power,

Acquaint thee with its dear familiar name?

Behold in *her* thy native earth.   How calm!

How beautiful in her serenity

She floats upon the blue empyrean flood!

Who could believe that underneath that calm

The tides of passion are awake?   We know

The sorrow and the sin that revel there,

Linked ever with the life of man—we know

What hollowness, and agony, and gloom,

The mantle of her beauty hides—but they

Whom Fate has made the tenants of this orb,

Unknowingly revere that earth as God—

Looking around with soul-less eyes, they see

The outward form and aspect, but forget

The inner life of things—That Mighty One

For what is all the spacious universe

With its proud splendour?   What the thousand shapes

Which fill the human héart with loveliness—

What are they but the presence of the Lord?

Divine conceptions of the beautiful,

Imperishable ever, and deep thoughts,

Coëval with the very being of God,

Embodied in the passive elements:

They have forgotten *him* who gave them birth,

And turned to worship idols.—Void of love,

Incapable of elevating faith,

They bow their hearts to a debasing creed

Of sensuality, and carnal rites

Which fill the soul with darkness.   But at length

The hour of chastisement arrives, and Fate

Implacable, with righteous vengeance armed,

Is pressing onward to its destined goal:

The young men see no visions, and the old

Dream not of woe and ruin, moving on

With wings of lightning speed—they shall behold

The meeting of these mighty combatants;

They shall behold their own eternal God

Vanish in dust and ashes from His sphere.

But see! Where from the city gates advance

The multitudes, thick swarming, self-deceived

With eager zeal; from every land they come,

To swell the great millennial festival

In honour of their moon; join thou the throng,

And follow where its evil guidance leads."

He spoke; already did the plain resound

With echoing steps and voices; with such speed

The crowd came on.   I saw in solemn pomp

Uncounted myriads pass by; distinct

In shape and hue, with vestures manifold,

Of their own regions: Diamond, and gold,

Rare spices, ivory, and fragrant wood,

With woven robes, and costly merchandize.

Unlike, and yet analogous to man,

The divers races did appear, as though

The children of the many climes of earth,

By some strange chance were gathered in one place;

Tartar, and Ethiopian, and the sons

Of silken Hindostan, Arab, and Copt,

The feathery chieftains of the Southern isles,

The men who drink of that Assyrian stream,

Euphrates, and the wild Caucasian tribes;

Together with the wide-spread progeny

Of those, who in the rough Hercynian wood

Went naked to the beating of the storm;

With all who till that mighty continent,

Which, drawing from the mountains, and the caves,

Innumerable complicated streams

Down their strong slopes to the recoiling sea,

Great Amazon, and Orinoco, drain,

And silver Plata with her double flood;
Araucan, Caribbean, and the men
Of Patagon, feigned of gigantic size:
Such was the aspect which these multitudes
Wore as they passed.   I followed in their train,
Until we reached a gently rising ground,
Where, mirrored in the soft and silent wave,
A massive temple stood, majestical
Above all human art; Such as might rise
Upon a poet's eye at dead of night,
If he that day alone had looked upon
The city of the sun—or, mightier yet,
The marble halls of Memphis in her pride;
Syene, or the wide magnificence
Of hundred-gated Thebes, with all her towers
And pyramids, fast by the river Nile;
Whilst yet, through every portal opening wide,
With bannered ornaments, and martial sound
Of echoing brass, the living tide of war
Flowed forth against the dusky kings who sat

In Meroë, and the continuous crowd
Of scythèd chariots, terrible in fight,
Came thundering through her peaceful obelisks.
All of black marble was this wondrous fane,
Spreading itself abroad in halls, and towers
Frequent with mighty columns, underneath
Vast cupolas of mournful majesty.
A pile like to the great metropolis
Of some slain warrior in cycles old,
When a whole people slaughtered on his tomb,
Accompanied unto the home of death
Their ghastly monarch, that he still might rule
The city of the silent—a dead king
Of a dead people, to eternity.
As we came on, under the gloomy walls,
Before the long procession open flowed
The adamantine gates—from either side
On noiseless hinges gliding from our path;
And nation after nation entered in.
The rich moss-agate framed the temple's floor,

Stretching far onward to the lustrous stair

Behind the crimson veil, which from above,

Fastened to dizzy pinnacles, and heights

Scarce visible, athwart the lofty hall

Hung waving like a sea, and hid from sight

The altar of the oracles, untrod

Save by the priest at the appointed hour.

Circling around, black marble galleries

On columns leant, whose palmy capitals

Were living adamant, intensely bright;

Whilst high above, around the solemn wall,

Sculptured with strange device, and traceries

More beautiful than those of Phidias old,

Huge windows of the purple amethyst

Tier above tier arose, and silently

Mellowed the day into a gloom divine,

Up to the very summit of the fane.

Between each lofty window's slumbrous shade,

Great stars of glowing emerald were set,

Serenely bright and calm, and narrow lines

Of diamond light, between each purple tier,

Ran round the great majestic cupola:

Such was the temple sacred to their Moon.

Along the glossy pavement of the hall

In solemn march continuous, one by one,

The banded tribes advanced—Before the veil

They knelt to offer up the splendid gifts,

Which their vain piety had brought to add

To all the sumless wealth (statues of gold,

Invaluable gems, bright thrones of pearl,

And chrysolite,) which lay unseen below;

Stored up in the ancestral treasuries

Of the great temple, from the days of old.

Nor wanted, as they passed, the sumptuous aid

Of false religion—all the glittering rites

Idolatrous, which captivate the sense;

Music, and light, and perfumes, and the swell

Of frequent hymns, and the protracted prayer,

With change of place, and vesture, and vain forms

Elaborate and perplexed—until the time

Of the last sacrifice, to be performed,

With an exceeding pomp and luxury,

To their bright Moon under the eye of heaven:

The high priest led the way, but suddenly

Upon the threshold stopped and shrieked aloud

With frantic voice and gesture.   Then I saw

All that immeasurable multitude,

Fluctuate like the sea—through the long files

Ran a low murmur of despair, and dread,

In the same breath of time, communicate

From man to man, like the electric fire:

Then, with a sudden impulse, from the fane,

Regardless of all order forth they ran,

Confused and masterless, filling the plains

With dissonant and savage screams of fear.

It was indeed an awful spectacle!

Onward it rolled, shedding around its path
Wide-ruining blasts, and flakes of raging fire,
Insufferably fierce and fast:—The moon
Glowed opposite, with mild and lovely light;
And the two worlds drew near—we saw them join;
Like some bright seraph, and the baleful fiend,
Meeting in mortal combat, on they came;
But we saw naught beyond—for, as they met,
From the dun skies closer and heavier fell
The sullen mist, and burning floods of smoke
Closed over us, making a denser night
Than the black vapour which was shed around
Christ crucified—or that more ancient gloom
When God with palpable thick darkness smote
Proud Egypt; and the monarch of the Nile
Trembled in sudden blindness on his throne;
But, not the less, through that gross atmosphere,
Impenetrable to the sight, there came
Strange thunderings; Ebbing and flowing sounds
Of wild uproar, like the convulsive crash

Of scattered elements in some far world.

Whilst louder than the thunders, heard above

The jar of the dissolving earth, a voice

Like the last trumpet of the Lord, arose,

Crying, "God has judged you in his wrath.   That Moon

Shall shine no more in heaven—false worshippers

Of a false God, repent ye of your sins."

PRUSSIC ACID.

SONG OF THE SPIRITS OF DEATH.

" FEVERISH and fierce, the hurrying crowd
  Can see no beauty in the tomb;
The eyeless skeleton, the shroud,
  Appal them into hopeless gloom;

" These are the wrecks of life—not Death,
  Before whose loveliness benign,
Each earthly sorrow vanisheth
  From all, who cross her calming line:

" Weak man with her identifies

    A scythèd monster, he miscalls ;

Still this is life, who as he flies,

    Turns back, to mock the wretch who falls.

" We know her, in another guise,

    Of deepening thought, and quiet love,

Serenely fair, divinely wise,

    And changeless as the heavens above.

" We know her, as the faithful spouse

    Of sleep from toil and evil free,

And around her pale and placid brows

    Wreath'd blossoms of the Almond-tree.

" She loves the flower, she loves the fruit,

    Because, within them hidden flows

An essence, rapid to transmute

    Man to the dim caves of repose.

" Loud-throated war is swift to kill,

    When cannon roar across the lea,

We honom *him*, but swifter still

    The noiseless work of the Almond-tree :

" The Lord of pain, the Lord of grief,

    Of fell despair, in it we see;

Proud Life is vassal to each leaf

    That flutters, from the Almond-tree.

" Pale genius, too forlorn to live,

    When rest and hope like sunlight flee,

Finds, what the laurel will not give,

    Upon its kindred Almond-tree.

" And wounded love, whose heart's blood flows,

    Like water searching out the sea,

May change its dead and scornèd rose

    For chaplets, from the Almond-tree.

That reverence for the Almond-tree."

LINES TO LADY * * * *

Lady, thou art very fair,

Safe under wings of tenderest care,

Youth her gayest dress doth wear,

   And life (as the warm summer day

Bends o'er a rose-bud lovingly,)

Breathes out her blessedness on thee.

Sorrow thou hast never known,

Rank and riches are thine own,

Thy mellow laughter's breezelike tone

   Chaseth all mists of gloom away ;

What cloud can stain the stars above ?

What sorrow quench thy lamp of love ?

And yet—though bright the prospect be,

Search well thy spirit's depth, to see

How thou canst bear calamity—

   Thou smilest, but I do not speak

Of warm affections chilled for life,

Of young hearts stabbed, as with a knife.

I do not speak of loveliness

Blighted by unforeseen distress,

Thy moments winged with pleasure, fly ;
Thou smilest, as the hours go by—
But thunder gathers in the sky :
    Wake from thy love-dream, wake, and see,
How troubled all things look, how strange,
How full of wickedness, and change.

Wild dreams of sin and strife abound,
Harsh voices mutter, with a sound
Like earthquakes moaning under ground.
    Yes! lovely one, I speak to thee,
Strengthen, and arm thy patient will,
To bear the fierce extremes of ill.

It may be, that my dazzled eye
Looks falsely on futurity ;
The stream may roll on peacefully ;
    Yet in thy mirth remember, how
Sunk down of old, the song, the dance,
When Ruin smote the land of France.

There was more pleasure there, more mirth,

Than over all the peopled earth;

But Time to a dark hour gave birth,

   And all at once, it seemed as though

Beneath some troop of dancers gay,

The painted floor had given way.

So fearfully, so suddenly,

From laughter, wealth, and luxury,

Down fell that proud nobility;

   Struck, as from cloudless skies, with flame,

Into a gulf of blood they fell,

And in their place uprose a hell.

Bright hair, in a few weary hours,

Whitened beneath its crown of flowers

In pleasure's own belovèd bowers;

Gore streamed, as from a fountain head,

The land was covered with the dead,

The young child with its mother bled,

   Unstained alike, and innocent,

And madness mixed itself with crime—

Read *thou* the annals of that time.

Read, and reflect, with earnest prayer,

Thy heart, for softness made, prepare,

Anguish more deep than death, to bear;

   Whatever then from God is sent,

Thy soul will be by him endued

With meek unfailing fortitude.

GENEVRA.

The feelings of Genevra's lover, on the body of his mistress being discovered, after a disappearance of half a century.

Vide ROGERS's Italy.

" THESE locks, which round my fingers twine,
    Are beautiful, and bright,
Such as they ever were—but mine
    Are withered, thin, and white.
Yet, when beneath the ilex shade,
    We pledged a fruitless vow;
They clustered, as in light arrayed,
    Around my youthful brow.
I was young then, who now am weak and old,
And this heart warm, which is so stern and cold.

Old as I am, thy mother's cries
   I have not yet forgot,
When, through the dusky galleries,
   We sought, and found thee not,
Till sportive wonder became fear,
   And laughing lips grew dumb;
For, though we called her far and near,
   The maiden did not come.
She had been seen by many, just before,
But the place knew her joyous laugh no more.

She must have withered, day by day,
   With friends for ever nigh—
She must have perished, where she lay,
   Still striving not to die.
For throbs of burning hope were given,
   (Till the last breath was gone)
Through that fierce anguish.—God in heave
   Was this a death for one
In whose young heart, so tender and so gay,
Love dwelt—as light inhabiteth the day.

How terrible the rise and fall
    Of soul-killing suspense!
I tore myself away from all,
    Upon some weak pretence;
I hid myself in darkness black,
    Upon the hard cold ground,
That I might hear, when I came back,
    " The lost one has been found."
I said unto my heart, why beatest thou?
Let me return—they *must* have found her now.

There met me, when at length I came,
    No such delightful sound;
I found, what I had left, the same
    Wan faces all around.
We struggled with our fears to cope,
    Throughout that restless day;
But all the while, the tide of hope
    Ebbed, drop by drop, away:
And when the sun went down beneath the sea,
We sunk under the weight of agony.

Now after fifty years of pain,

　　And toil, by sea, and land :

I look upon my bride again,

　　I touch the loved-one's hand :

And all the dreary gulf between

　　Thy last kiss, and this hour,

Is like some dim fantastic scene,

　　When night and sleep have power.

All is confused within me—and I seem

About to wake, from some distressing dream.

ENOCH.

———

" A THOUSAND years have faded like a dream
    Since the first birth of time ;
On either side of our Assyrian stream
    Unnumbered cities climb,

" With obelisks and heaven-searching spires,
    The blue abysmal sky ;
On altars of rich carving, perfumed fires
    Are tended carefully :

" And ever in the marble colonnades,
    And streets as sunshine bright,
With melodies of love, our bright-haired maids
    Quicken the dreamful night:

" And smiles are interchanged, without control,
    With full and happy sighs;
New lights have dawned upon the human soul,
    And taught it to be wise.

" How would our ancient father, full of woes,
    Rejoice that it is so,
Had not the thing within, which feels, and knows,
    Fled from him like a foe;

" We too, his children, must like him bow down
    To that abhorred power;
Alas! no maiden's smile, no warrior's frown,
    Can wring from it *one* hour.

" Even now, to think of *Death*, who mixes grief
 With all things that delight;
Our seared hearts tremble, as the sapless leaf
 Shakes in an eastern blight.

" Oh! that some spirit mild, and wise, and good,
 Would teach us how to keep
The life for ever young within the blood;
 Secure of that chill sleep;

" Then should we never suddenly let fall
 The wine-cup at our lips;
Then should we live, and love, together all,
 In mirth without eclipse.

" Thou art a prophet, father; call aloud,
 Unto the God of truth,
That he may chase this overhanging cloud,
 From the bright skies of youth:

" How can the Lord of mercy vex mankind
    With knowledge such as this,
When every living thing around is blind
    In unalarmèd bliss?

" Like one pale coward, who trembles in a host
    Of heroes flushed with hope,
When the shrill trumpet-sound is tossed
    Down some long grassy slope—

" Like one unwelcome guest, in some bright hall
    Thronged with the beautiful,
Who troubleth all that gorgeous festival
    With aspect strange and dull,

" Such, amid all the merriment, and bliss,
    Which this life furnisheth,
The many joys of love, and wine, is *this*,
    The single thought of death.

To fill thy home with gold."

Thus amid moonlit palaces, and towers,
    And columned halls of pride,
The young and gay, crowned with ambrosial flowers,
    Spoke sad, and downward-eyed;

They spoke to one, who sat upon the ground,
    Under a cypress tree,
And heard, or seemed to hear, the heavy sound
    Of an outbursting sea.

The noise of mighty waters, evermore
    Smote on his throbbing ears;
In sleep he heard unearthly screams, which tore
    His lonely soul with fears:

Fell on him like a cloud.

Thus his mind hung upon futurity,
    In that all-evil time,
And saw, by heaven unrolled, before her lie
    The map of human crime.

A secret influence, like wasting flame,
    Withered him day and night,
Till every thing he used to love, became
    As nothing in his sight.

Strength melted from his mighty limbs, and sleep
 Touched not his burning eye;
Often he sat, without the power to weep,
 And only prayed to die.

Alas! no earthly spirit can sustain,
 By her inherent force,
Without convulsions of oppressive pain,
 That awful intercourse:

Before all worlds, was it appointed so,
 That it could not be given
To man, but with *such* agonies, to know
 The secret things of heaven.

But at that time, the supernatural dread—
 The spirit's secret chill—
Before some power of gentleness had fled,
 Leaving him calm, and still.

All motionless had he been stretched for hours,
    Under the deepening shade,
Dreaming of Eden's amaranthine bowers,
    In heaven's own light arrayed:

The stars came out above that lonely place,
    The river gurgled on,
The breeze played round and round his haggard face,
    As if its task were done.

The gentle influence of declining day
    Melted into his breast;
The balmy moonlight soothed him, and he lay
    Cradled in perfect rest.

Why do the sons of pleasure strive to break
    That brief hour of repose?
Why, with these idle questionings, awake
    His deep heart to its woes?

Lapped in such joys to live?

Have they not satisfied, and filled the soul,

With all that earth can give?

No! there are memories which ache and burn,

And bitter tears to flow;

In each light-seeming heart, a shrouded urn,

Sacred to love and woe.

They had asked answering looks, from eyes now dead,

Hands they had clasped, were bone;

Out of their path belovèd things had fled,

Into a world unknown.

Day after day, their forced and fitful mirth

Sunk into deeper gloom,

Until, to all alike, the glad warm earth

Seemed rayless, as the tomb.

Then came they from the feast, in blank despair,
    Seeking that lonely seer ;
As if there needed but a prophet's prayer
    To quench sorrow, and fear.

Alas! the mind which in its anguish flies
    Still to the joys of earth,
To nought, but hollow sensualities,
    And grovelling hope, gives birth.

They prayed, as if the deep laws of the sky,
    Which in God's heart abide,
Coëval with his own eternity,
    Could *thus* be set aside :

As if the Lord, that Spirit pure and just,
    Who sees the soul within,
Would give immortal life to this vile dust,
    Or happiness to sin.

pangs, on which no human eye could look,
Beneath some touch of power,
prophet's mighty stature reeled and shook,
Like an imperial tower,

ch feels the earthquake, raging underground
Against its marble root, ·
lst the calm air above it, and around,
Stirs not the ripened fruit.

rooding stillness covered all things near,
As if before a storm,
il, like evil spirits, Pain and Fear
Fled from his stately form.

Then, as the dead upon a field of fight,
    After a hard-fought day,
That impious multitude, in dumb affright,
    Around the prophet lay.

His keen eye, sharper than a two-edged sword,
    Smote on them from afar;
On his high front, the presence of the Lord
    Sat like a burning star.

He spoke of those unquiet souls, which lie
    Fast bound in chains of clay;
Of the strong hope of immortality
    Thrown, like a weed, away;

Till all high aspirations, one by one,
    Fade from the darkened heart;
As those brief splendours, which outlive the sun,
    From the grey clouds depart.

" The world," he said, " beyond their senses dim,
    The realm of upper air,
Invisible to all on earth, but him,
    Before his eye lay bare."

Often, he said, with a deep sense of awe,
    His heart within him died,
Rebuked by some high presence; and he saw
    A spirit at his side:

And voices of strange music hovered near,
    Denouncing death and woe;
Or demon laughters jarred upon his ear,
    In mocking cadence slow.

He told them, how before his trancèd eye,
    From morn to eventide,

" Let loose the wild winds in their destined flight,
　　For I, the Lord, must sweep
The offending sons of Adam from my sight:
　　Let loose the raging deep."

The prophet paused—an awful shadow smote
　　The flower-enamelled sod—
A sound there was, as thunder heard remote,
　　And Enoch walked with God.

ODE ON THE FALL OF POLAND.

Poland has fallen! Heaven! how long
    Shall fraud and tyranny be strong?
How long shall Russia's impious lord be free
    To trample on the hearts of men,
That he may turn, with smiles of savage glee,
    To revel in his Arctic den?
What! must the sword of righteous vengeance sleep?
Must the warm heart its even tenor keep?
    And shroud its feelings from the light,
    And veil its horror and affright,
    Lest we should rouse the Muscovite?

Alas! how great is England's fall;

Was it for *this* she smote the Gaul?

And poured her blood, like summer rain,

Upon the burning fields of Spain?

Is it to this barbaric race

That the fierce Corsican gave place?

Alas! old Warsaw's crumbling wall

Startled no echo in its fall:

Though Poland flung her banners forth,

Against the millions of the north:

And faced the slaves, who rushed to slay,

Like some proud forest-stag at bay,

In foreign lands, no answering shout

From nations burst in thunder out;

No people started from their rest,

No trumpet sounded in the west;

That high and holy enterprise

Awoke no feeling, but surprise.

The hatred ceasing but with life,

The fierce roar of the rapid strife,

The smoke, the death-fires covering all around,

    As though from some volcano cast,

The heavy tramp, that shook the heated ground,

    As if an earthquake past,

  The axe of vengeance raised and bare,

      The despot's panting haste to smite,

The high hearts breaking in despair,

    As the last column sunk in fight,

On Europe's languid senses fell,

Like a theatric spectacle;

Yea; as in some luxurious room,

    We fix our rapt and earnest eyes

On scenes, which some great limner's sight,

In darkness saw by its own light,

Wild paintings full of death and gloom,

Like dreams arrested in their flight;

    Yet feel no human sympathies

For the pale forms within, which seem

Convulsed in suffering's fierce extreme,

So gazed the sons of Europe all
On that brave land's disastrous fall.

Alone they stood, alone they fell,
Sprung from those knights, to God, and Europe true,
Whose war-cry well the Turkish Spahi knew,
Whose coursers, as the tameless eagle, flew,
Whose spears, like fire set to grass, broke through
      The masses of the infidel ;
And gave to death the turbaned lord
Of many an Asiatic horde,
When from the East, with fierce acclaim,
The children of the Crescent came,
Like locusts warping on the wind,
To leave despair and death behind.

Alone they stood, alone they fell ;
For many a month, the cannon's roar
      Boomed from old Warsaw's citadel ;
For many a month, with earthquake sound,
The hoofs of charging horsemen tore

The bloody turf around :
And still untamed, from day to day,
They kept the northern wolf away,
　But help in none was found.
Instead of filling heaven and earth
With the loud trumpet's awful mirth ;
Instead of pouring to the breeze
A shout, like the awakened seas ;
Instead of pressing to the strife,
Like lightnings bursting into life ;
Instead of leaping on the foe
As leaps the eager lawine-snow ;
All fawned around the man of blood ;
All fawned around him, as he stood
On freedom stiffening in her gore,
With his foul triumph crimsoned o'er.
Even now the threat of vengeance is deferred,
　No people breathes a single word ;
　　Though still within that stately city,
The sob of breaking hearts is heard,

For the tyrant has no pity;

The buoyant hope, the keen desire,

Which filled the souls of all with fire;

Now to the eye doth seem,

The shadow of an unremembered dream;

Silent, and cold, like some deep frozen stream,

Which none would deem to be the rill,

That in the golden summer's beam,

With gurgling rush, and dazzling gleam,

Leapt joyously from hill to hill.

Alike on every spirit press

Deep lassitude and hopelessness;

Alike, by day and night, on all

The Tartar's iron scourges fall.

The vassal, on the ravaged wold

Sighs for the glorious deeds of old :

He sighs in secret, to behold

The downfall of his country's pride,

Wherewith, he was identified;

He mourns, because his native lord,

The son of an heroic name,

(Now fading, like an unfed flame)

Is forced, even as the idle foam

Shifts in the changing gale, to roam

    With crest defaced, and useless sword,

An exile from his ruined home :

The warworn noble must endure,

    In bitterness of heart, to see

The axe of ruthless vengeance laid,

    To his ancestral tree ;

Beneath whose venerable shade,

In all the pomp of age displayed,

    The peasant slept secure :

See that young mother, trembling there,

Pale, as a statue of despair.

What recks she, that like death around

The harsh blast strikes the lifeless ground ?

To her intense, and cureless grief,

Such outward suffering, is relief.

See! how with feeble steps and slow,

She tracks, along the frozen snow,

The crowded wain, wherein is borne,

From arms of clasping fondness torn,

The child of some historic stem,

Who might have worn a diadem.

Perchance the fairest flower of all,

The life of some ancestral hall,

She moved, like light, to cheer and bless,

A very star of loveliness :

Who tore that child of hope away?

Who turned those locks of gold to grey?

Who pierced that heart of love from far,

And outraged nature thus?   The Czar!

Alas! alas! for Poland's fate;

Her castles now are desolate;

Each city, is a place of tears,

The home of woe, and killing fears;

O'er her wide meadows, like a blight,

Hath swept the ruthless Muscovite :

Her bravest children wake to weep

    Their ruined country's woe,

Where the cold skies of northern Asia steep

    The trackless plains in snow :

    On wilds above, in mines below,

      The mark of servile scorn ;

    Forbid o'er Poland's fate to sigh,

    Too proud to sink, too brave to die,

      From Poland, and from glory, torn,

      They live, forgotten, and forlorn.

No more, as in the days of old, no more

    Does God fight visibly for martyrs here :

Our dim eyes reach not to the happy shore,

    Beyond time's clouded ocean moaning near:

Therefore it is, that round my spirit cling,

Dejection deep as death, forlorn dismay,

And heaviness, that will not pass away.

      We cannot in our blindness see,

      What will, what ought to be ;

We cannot soar on angel's wing,

Above the atmosphere of doubt and gloom,

Which makes this wide earth darker than the tomb,

Into that upper air,

Where all is bright and fair ;

The soul is fettered to a heavy doom,

Which it must learn to bear :

But still, the eyes of Heaven do not sleep,

The wisdom of the universe is deep ;

Though all around be dark, 'tis not for man

The footsteps of the Lord to scan :

What though we cannot shape the lightning's way,

To scare the tiger from his prey ?

What though we dare not say,

That heaven will rain down vengeance from above,

On those who draw the sword to slay ?

It is enough to know, that God is love,

And wiser than the sons of clay.

SYMPATHY.

The dew-drop is a trivial thing,
   Yet it lends freshness to the rose,
When diamonds, from the sun would fling,
   New withering on her wan repose.

With pride of their own lustre fired,
   The unloving gems burn on in vain;
The humble dew-drop, love inspired,
   Can wake the flower to life again.

Judge not a gift from outward show,
   Nor test it by its actual worth;
These are its body, far below,
   Its soul, is that which gives it birth.

TO TWO SISTER BRIDES,

WHO WERE MARRIED ON THE SAME DAY,

———

Not surely to unmix'd delight,
   Not to unhesitating mirth,
These trembling veils of virgin white
   And bridal orange-flowers give birth.

In the same cradle ye have slept
   The sleep that only childhood may,
Together smiled, together wept,
   Together knelt, and learned to pray.

Together !—in that solemn word
  What depth of love, what meaning lies;
It is, as if the heart were stirred
  By angel hymns from Paradise.

And now these twin-like years are o'er,
  These clasping tendrils disentwined,
Your thoughts and hopes can flow no more
  As channelled in a single mind.

Behind you, shifting rapidly
  As the wild rack beneath the blast,
In mazy movement, flutter by
  The dream-like tissues of the past.

Before you, full of mystery,
  Ages unborn their shadows fling;
Time, with its seed eternity,
  Sleeps in each slender marriage ring.

What marvel, then, that as ye kneel,
　　There fall some consecrating tears,
That dizzily ye seem to feel
　　The motion of the moving spheres?

But though dim shapes the air may fill,
　　One spot of heaven smiles above,
Through which, with lustre calm and still,
　　Shines on your hearts, the star of love.

And wider yet, from day to day
　　That stainless spot on high, shall spread;
And yet more full, love's deathless ray,
　　Cover with light each graceful head.

Cold were the man whose eyes could rest
　　On this beloved and lovely pair,
Nor feel within his thrilling breast,
　　A gush of blessing and of prayer.

Ay, coldert han the sunless north—
  Than the frore gale that numbs the sea—
The heart that is not rushing forth,
  Like brooks, by sudden spring set free.

Not such the multitudes, who press
  To look upon you once again,
In reverential tenderness,
  And tears, half pleasure and half pain.

Oh, priceless tribute! these are they
  Whose lives were soothed and raised by you;
On whom your gentle presence lay,
  As upon flowers, the evening dew.

Their loss they know, yet it is borne
  Without a touch of selfish fear;
Albeit, as if the spring were torn
  For ever, from the rolling year.

Not human hearts alone—the skies
    (Nor over dark, nor over bright),
Are clad in mystic sympathies,
    Of tender gloom, and chastened light.

So mild the sun, so soft the grey,
    It almost seems, as if there were
A spirit, in the silent day—
    A feeling, on the lifeless air:

As if these lawns and woodlands, full
    Of a deep instinct, resting not,
Motioned away the beautiful,
    In loving sadness, to their lot.

Yes—and for both that lot shall glow
    With splendours, not the gift of time;
Keeping undimmed, through weal and woe,
    The promise of its maiden prime.

High hopes are thine, oh! eldest flower,
   Great duties to be greatly done;
To soothe, in many a toil-worn hour,
   The noble heart which thou hast won.

Covet not then the rest of those,
   Who sleep through life unknown to fame;
Fate grants not passionless repose
   To her, who weds a glorious name.

He presses on through calm and storm
   Unshaken, let what will betide;
Thou hast an office to perform,
   To be his answering spirit bride.

The path appointed for his feet,
   Through desert wilds, and rocks may go,
Where the eye looks in vain to greet
   The gales, that from the waters blow.

Be thou a balmy breeze to him,

A fountain singing at his side;

A star, whose light is never dim,

A pillar, to uphold and guide.

Nay, haply, not of thee alone,

This proud futurity is true;

Wreaths, on as green a laurel grown,

To thy bright sister may be due.

Your happy destiny has been,

To find another tie in them,

Who might have rudely rushed between

The sister roses on the stem.

Like double stars, the even beam

Of their young glory burns on you;

So that the nearer heart may deem

Her own, the brighter of the two.

Let this yet more your souls unite,
  Into one woven thought and will;
Reflecting, like twin mirrors, light
  And beauty on each other still.

TO LEONORA.

It is a joy and blessing to behold
    Maidens of such ethereal mood,
Ripening, amid the smiles of young and old,
    Into the bloom of womanhood.

I saw thee, moving like a seraph's bride,
    Serenely gay in quiet grace;
And marked, on thine own river's grassy side,
    The beauty of that thoughtful face.

The native warmth of feelings, pure and deep,
    Alternating with graceful glee,
The souls of all, within thy sphere, did steep
    In fond, and yearning love, for thee.

The meekness of a spirit without strife,
    A heart from grief and passion free,
Just showed how beautiful a thing, the life
    So wasted here on earth, might be.

I see thee in a different scene to-night,
    Hurried along in pleasure's round ;
A thousand lamps have filled the air with light,
    Rich flowers are dropping to the ground.

In me the dance, in me this painted room,
    With all its empty forms of mirth,
To nothing, but a sense of smothered gloom,
    And heaviness of heart, gives birth.

Thou too its chilling influence hast proved;
   Thy smiles as yet their sweetness keep,
But not their sunny flash; the voice I loved,
   Though musical, is not so deep.

Oh thou, whom all things flatter and caress,
   Take heed lest meaner thoughts invade
That soul of reverential tenderness,
   For all, which the high God has made.

Fly from this scene of jealousy and strife,
   The realms where vanity has power:
This joyless and unprofitable life,
   Suits not so delicate a flower.

To thy old feelings, and old haunts, return;
   The woods—the streams—the ocean flood—
And the undying stars of night, which burn
   Like seraphs in the house of God.

TO THE MEMORY OF A DEAR FRIEND.

In our dim eyes too often doth it seem,

As if the Architect of earthly life

Built, only to pull down—the burning lamp

Of genius, in the very dawn of youth,

And love, and happiness, before its orb,

Has gathered strength to shed a deathless light

Upon the drear gloom of humanity,

Feels the chill blast of death, and vanishes

In the shadowy silence of the past.

The star is quenched by Him who framed its sphere,

When it begins to shine.—The forest oak,

Nurtured, and cherished long, in one short moment

Is smitten by God's thunder into dust.

The temple of the soul, elaborate

In splendour, and endowed with glorious gifts,

At once, as if in sport, is overthrown

By the same hand that raised it, leaving here

Sorrow that dieth not.—Friend of my youth,

Lamented spirit of lost excellence,

Thus has it been with thee!—the intellect,

Whose light was rising like a sun—the heart

Instinct with love, together have sunk down

Into the darkness of the sepulchre.

Alas! for those who watched thee with deep love,

Who knew thee as thou wert—and daily said,

When will his spirit open her strong wings,

Scaling the heaven of fame? when shall we see

His name, engraven among those which shine

Imperishable, with a starry fire

Piercing the sullen mists of death and time?

It is indeed a heavy blow—but yet

Not altogether sorrowful—not bare

Of solemn consolation.—If we turn

To the old time, and picture to ourselves

The loss of a dear friend, we shall be taught

How light our burden is.—Everything then

Ended with life—the proud philosopher

Smiled in derision at the blessed hope

Of immortality, and endless love

Among the spirits of departed men,

Coldly repeating, " Let us eat and drink,

To-morrow we shall die."—The poet's soul,

Feeding on melancholy thoughts of death,

And dull annihilation in the tomb,

Envied the falling flowers, and rotting leaves,

Their annual life.—Under the mellow light

Of sunset, on the warm Sicilian sea—

Under the moon, and the ethereal ray

Of the clear stars, amid the works of God,

Unconscious of his own high destiny,

He walked, musing uncomforted, and drew

From the chill Stygian fountain of despair,

The yearning pathos of his deathless verse.

Alas! how hopeless then, the pilgrimage

Of life, how sharp and terrible the stroke

Sundering the bonds of love!—We should have stood

Over his early tomb, and scattered flowers

To perish, and shed perfumes on the ground:

With a vain providence we should have called

The dews of heaven, to keep for ever.green

The consecrated spot, and bid the winds

Breathe low and deep around; we should have prayed

The Naiades and Dryads, to respect

The silence of his everlasting sleep.

Finding, alas! in prayers and hopes like these

A feeble solace and a last resource

For the rich fund of tenderness, and love,

Which, baffled as it was, in the warm heart

Lay undecayed, and inexhaustible.

Owning the horrible supremacy

Of death, over the hopes and joys of man,

We should have clung to the delights of earth,

Anchoring our hearts on sensuality,

And the low pleasures of this mortal state,

To spare ourselves such woe.—With dust, and mud,

We should have choked the fount of love within,

That its deep waters might be vexed no more.

How miserable! happier far to know

The word of Heaven, to be empowered to say,

Not in the grave, not in the loathsome pit

Of darkness, is the friend we love entombed.

He lives in God—through life, unstained like him,

Let us pass, comforting the heart with hope

Of meeting, in the sunny land of souls.

A COMMON PROSPECT.

How strange it must be without any pain,
   To lie upon the bed of death;
As the last pulses thrill each languid vein,
   And the lip trembles yet with breath:

Whilst the clear spirit, all unchanged within,
   Looks back along life's eddying stream,
And feels reality at length begin,
   After a long and fevered dream.

That scene made up of darkness, and of light,
    The irrecoverable past,
Like a great picture lies before our sight,
    Seen all at once from first to last.

Its hopes, its passions, its events, we see,
    Its acts of hate, and fear, and love,
Just as the gate of immortality
  ˙ Turns on its golden hinge above.

Some think of time alone, to others life
    Is the porch of eternity :
In that last hour of inward calm, or strife,
    How awful must the difference be !

SONNET

WRITTEN IN THE FIRST PAGE OF WORDSWORTH'S POEMS.

In this high poet's song, you will not find
Fierce passion painted with a demon's force,
Vice, by wild incongruities refined,
And every virtue poisoned at its source.
Nor yet, markĕd by strange hatred of mankind,
The drunken anguish of a false remorse :
His soul is calm and lofty as a star,
Nor does he sing to give his spirit rest,
And charm to peace the hell within his breast.
But as a quiet lake reflects from far,
The forests, and the mountains, and the sky ;
Thus, led by nature as a loving nurse,
His mind is made her mirror, and his verse
Is full of hope, and immortality.

SONNET.

You spake of reason, of reality,

As if high monuments of mental power

Were nought but dreams, to be thrown idly by,

Just glanced at, and forgotten in an hour.

A hollow creed, and false philosophy,

For one so pure and beautiful to hold.

Let others phantom-following, strive in vain,

To make those mocking visions, fame and gold,

A haven and a resting-place for life.

But live not thou with thine own heart at strife,

To build up *that* in beauty, without stain,

Is the true end of being—and God has given,

(Lest the soul faint in weariness and pain,)

Ethereal wings, to lift her up to heaven.

SONNET

THE poet, is like one by fancy led,

Whose footsteps in the lonely morning press

Some stubborn hill of difficult access,

Which seems to lengthen on above his head,

As though it sported with his weariness.

His path is steeped in vapour dark as death,

And flooded with chill mist—whilst to and fro

Thousands, along the dusty road beneath,

Securely in bright sunshine come and go:

But, ever and anon, in that steep way

The sudden mountain gales, with joyous breath,

Uproot the seated clouds—the sun's warm ray

Leaps forth, and on wide plains below are thrown

Ethereal splendours, seen by him alone.

SONNET TO PERDITA,

ON THE OCCASION OF SENDING HER A TRIFLING PRESENT

A MOMENTARY wish passed through my brain,

To be the monarch of a magic place

Thick sown with burning gems, or to constrain

The uncouth help of some half-demon race,

Vexing the pearl-paved hollows of the main

For thee, and starry caverns in far space :

It was a wish unwisely formed, and vain ;

Even in the humblest trifles, love can trace

That which no mine can give, no Genii's wing

From depths beneath, or heights above can bring,

The memories of each kind look and tone,

Gestures, and glancing smiles, into the gift

Pass like a living spirit, and uplift

Its value, to the level of their own.

HIGH strains and pure, worthy to live and shine
By their own light hereafter, still in these
I find not what I sought, ye ancient seas,
And matchless rivers, Forests of dark pine,
And of each tree that fires the autumn breeze
With myriad quivering colours, bright as gold,
Maple and beech, and leagues of clustering vine,
Round huge hill-shrouding oaks, that have grown old
Unmarked, save by the changeless stars divine,
There come from you no solemn presences
Shaping the hearts of men—no spirit glides
From the vast woods at night, no marvellous dreams
Flow from the sullen shade, in whom abides
The sceptre of the ever-sounding streams.

SONNET

It cannot be; the effort to transfuse

Into dead, measured form, this setting sun,

With its rich harmony of living hues,

Painter and bard alike would wisely shun :

We may not hope to reach that mighty one,

The Prince and Chief of Authors, who imbues

This ancient heaven, bright earth, and stainless sea,

With a more deep and wondrous poesy.

Creator—Maker—Poet—is *his* name,

Not ours, who struggle painfully to climb,

Clothed only with the shadow of the same.

Whilst He on visionary heights sublime

Sits fathomless of soul, and placidly

Keeps weaving on his giant epic—Time.

---

his poem is intended to illustrate the spirit of York-
racing, now unhappily, or happily, as the case may
on the decline. The perfect acquaintance of every
on the ground, with the pedigrees, performances,
characters of the horses engaged—his genuine interest
he result—and the mixture of hatred and contempt
h he used to feel for the Newmarket favourites, who
down to carry off his great national prize, must be
known to everybody who has ever crossed the Trent in
ust or September :—altogether it constituted a peculiar
fication of English feeling, which I thought deserved

to be recorded; and in default of a more accomplished Pindar, I have here endeavoured to do so.

THE sun is bright, the sky is clear,
    Above the crowded course,
As the mighty moment draweth near
    Whose issue shows *the horse.*
The fairest of the land are here
To watch the struggle of the year,
The dew of beauty and of mirth,
Lies on the living flowers of earth,
And blushing cheek and kindling eye
Lend brightness to the sun on high:
And every corner of the north,
Has poured her hardy yeomen forth;
The dweller by the glistening rills
That sound among the Craven hills;
The stalwart husbandman who holds
His plough upon the eastern wolds;

The sallow shrivelled artisan,

Twisted below the height of man,

Whose limbs and life have mouldered

Within some foul and clouded town,

Are gathered thickly on the lea,

Or streaming from far homes to see

If Yorkshire keeps her old renown;

Or if the dreaded Derby horse

Can tear the larrel from her course;

With the same look in every face,

The same keen feeling, they retrace

The legends of each ancient race:

Recalling Reveller in his pride,

Or Blacklock of the mighty stride,

Or listening to some grey-haired sage

Full of the dignity of age;

How, neither pace, nor length, could

Old Muley Moloch's speed and fire;

How Hambletonian beat of yore

Such racers, as are seen no more;

How Yorkshire coursers, swift as they,

Would leave this southern horse half way,

But that the creatures of to-day,

Are cast in quite a different mould,

From what he recollects of old.

Clear peals the bell; (at that known sound),

Like bees, the people cluster round;

On either side upstarting then

One thick dark wall of breathing men,

Far down as eye can stretch, is seen

Along yon vivid strip of green,

Where keenly watched by countless eyes,

'Mid hopes, and fears, and prophecies,

Now fast, now slow, now here, now there,

With hearts of fire, and limbs of air,

Snorting and prancing—sidling by

With arching neck, and glancing eye,

In every shape of strength and grace,

The horses gather for the race;

Soothed for a moment all, they stand

Together, like a sculptured band,

Each quivering eyelid flutters thick,

Each face is flushed, each heart beats quick;

And all around dim murmurs pass,

Like low winds moaning on the grass.

Again—the thrilling signal sound—

And off at once, with one long bound,

Into the speed of thought they leap,

Like a proud ship rushing to the deep.

A start! a start! they're off, by heaven,

Like a single horse, though twenty-seven,

And mid the flash of silks we scan

A Yorkshire jacket in the van;

            Hurrah! for the bold bay mare!

I'll pawn my soul her place is there

    Unheaded to the last,

For a thousand pounds, she wins unpast—

           Hurrah! for the matchless mare!

A hundred yards have glided by
　And they settle to the race,
More keen becomes each straining eye,
　More terrible the pace.
Unbroken yet o'er the gravel road
Like maddening waves the troop has flowed,
　　　　　But the speed begins to tell.
And Yorkshire sees, with eye of fear,
The Southron stealing from the rear.
　　　　　Ay! mark his action well!
Behind he is, but what repose!
How steadily and clean he goes!
What latent speed his limbs disclose!
What power in every stride he shows!
They see, they feel, from man to man
The shivering thrill of terror ran,
And every soul instinctive knew
It lay between the mighty two.
The world without, the sky above,
　Have glided from their straining eyes—

Future and past, and hate and love,

    The life that wanes, the friend that dies.

Even grim remorse, who sits behind

Each thought and motion of the mind,

These now are nothing, Time and Space

Lie in the rushing of the race;

As with keen shouts of hope and fear

They watch it in its wild career.

Still far a-head of the glittering throng,

Dashes the eager mare along,

And round the turn, and past the hill,

Slides up the Derby winner still.

The twenty-five that lay between

Are blotted from the stirring scene,

And the wild cries which rang so loud,

Sink by degrees throughout the crowd,

To one deep humming, like the roar

Of swollen seas on a northern shore.

In distance dwindling to the eye

Right o_posite the stand the lie

And scarcely seem to stir ;

Though an Arab scheich his wives would give

For a single steed, that with them could live

Three hundred yards, without the spur.

But though so indistinct and small,

You hardly see them move at all,

There are not wanting signs, which show

Defeat is busy as they go.

Look how the mass, which rushed away

As full of spirit as the day,

So close compacted for a while,

Is lengthening into single file.

Now inch by inch it breaks, and wide

And spreading gaps the line divide.

As forward still, and far away

Undulates on the tired array

Gay colours, momently less bright,

Fade flickering on the gazer's sight,

Till keenest eyes can scarcely trace

The onward ripple of the race.

Care sits on every lip and brow.

" Who leads? who fails? how goes it now?"

One shooting spark of life intense,

One throb of refluent suspense,

And a far rainbow-coloured light

Trembles again upon the sight.

Look to yon turn! Already there

Gleams the pink and black of the fiery mare,

And through *that*, which was but now a gap,

Creeps on the terrible white cap.

Uprises straight a quivering shout

Wrung from their fevered spirits out,

And runs like fire along the sod,

" He's there! he's coming up, by G—!"

Then momently like gusts, you heard,

" He's sixth—he's fifth—he's fourth—he's third;"

As on, like some arrowy meteor-flame,

The stride of the Derby winner came.

And during all that anxious time,

Sneer as it suits you at m   ıh me)

The earnestness became sublime;

Common and trite as is the scene

At once, so thrilling, and so mean,

To him who strives his heart to scan,

And feels the brotherhood of man,

That needs *must* be a mighty minute,

When a crowd has but one soul within it.

As some bright ship with every sail

Obedient to the urging gale,

Darts by vext hulls, which side by side,

Dismasted on the raging tide,

Are struggling onward, wild and wide,

Thus, through the reeling field he flew,

And near, and yet more near he drew;

Each leap seems longer than the last,

Now—now—the second horse is past,

And the keen rider of the mare,

With haggard looks of feverish care,

Hangs forward on the speechless air,

By steady stillness nursing in

The remnant of her speed to win.

One other bound—one more—'tis done;

Right up to her the horse has run,

And head to head, and stride for stride

Newmarket's hope, and Yorkshire's pride,

Like horses harnessed side by side,

   Are struggling to the goal.

Ride! gallant son of Ebor, ride!

For the dear honour of the north,

Stretch every bursting sinew forth,

   Put out thy inmost soul,—

And with knee, and thigh, and tightened rein,

Lift in the mare by might and main;

The feelings of the people reach,

What lies beyond the springs of speech,

So that there rises up no sound

From the wide human life around;

One spirit flashes from each eye,

One impulse lifts each heart throat-high,

One short and panting silence broods,

O'er the wildly-working multitudes,

As on the struggling coursers press,

So deep the eager silentness,

That underneath their feet the turf

Seems shaken, like the eddying surf

    When it tastes the rushing gale,

And the singing fall of the heavy whips,

Which tear the flesh away in strips,

    As the tempest tears the sail,

On the throbbing heart and quivering ear,

Strike vividly distinct, and near.

But hark! what a rending shout was there,

" He's beat! he's beat!—by heaven, the mare!"

Just on the post she springs away

At once, from thirty thousand throats

   Rushes the Yorkshire roar,

And the name of their northern winner floats

   A league from the course, and more.

―――――――

" FOR our martyred Charles I pawned my plate

   For his son I spent my all,

That a churl might dine, and drink my wine,

   And preach in my father's hall:

That father died on Marston Moor,

   My son on Worcester plain;

But the king he turned his back on me,

   When he got his own again.

" The other day, there came, God wot!
    A solemn pompous ass,
Who begged to know if I did not go
    To the sacrifice of mass:
I told him fairly to his face,
    That in the field of fight,
I had shouted loud for church and king,
    When he would have run outright.

" He talked of the Man of Babylon
    With his rosaries and copes,
As if a Roundhead wasn't worse
    Than half a hundred Popes.
I don't know what the people mean,
    With their horror and affright;
All Papists that I ever knew
    Fought stoutly for the right.

" Then spur and sword, was the battle word,
    And we made their helmets ring,
Howling, like madmen, all the while,
    For God, and for the king.
And though they snuffled psalms, to give
    The Rebel-dogs their due,
When the roaring-shot poured close and hot,
    They were stalwart men and true.

" On the fatal field of Naseby,

    Where Rupert lost the day,

By hanging on the flying crowd

    Like a lion on his prey,

I stood and fought it out, until,

    In spite of plate and steel,

The blood that left my veins that day,

    Flowed up above my heel.

" And certainly, it made those quail

    Who never quailed before,

To look upon the awful front

    Which Cromwell's horsemen wore.

I felt that every hope was gone,

    When I saw their squadrons form,

And gather for the final charge,

    Like the coming of the storm.

Oh ! where was Rupert in that hour
  Of danger, toil, and strife :
It would have been to all brave men,
  Worth a hundred years of life,
To have seen that black and gloomy force,
  As it poured down in line,
Met midway by the Royal horse,
  And Rupert of the Rhine.

THE EAGLE'S NEST.

THESE VERSES WERE SUGGESTED BY AN INCIDENT REL

IN "WILD SPORTS OF THE WEST."

" Speed hither, all my vassals bold,
    And in the brown rock's caverned breast,
Where yon huge fissure yawns, behold
    The ocean eagle's nest.

" The waves beneath in thunder fling
    Unbroken leagues of angry foam ;
Above, with iron beak and wing,
    The Osprey wheels around her home.

" Five hundred feet of sheer ascent,
  As metal darkly smooth and bare,
No jutting stone, no twig is lent
  To help the cragsman there.

" Who boasts a fearless heart, and limbs
  Like the wild cat, or mountain roe,
An eye that neither winks nor swims,
  Though the waves dance and shine below ?

" Who in that rush, and whirl and glare,
  A pulse unhurried can maintain ;
And face the mother-bird's despair,
  With steady hand and brain?"

In air the chosen vassal stands,
  Down swinging on his venturous quest;
Now, now he touches it, his hands
  Scrape round the unprotected nest.

M

" Up with him, friends, in pride and mirth !
   Up with the rope, the prize is won !"—
Won is it ?—no—by heaven and earth
   His task is but begun !

With claws fast clenched, and eyes that gleam
   Like light'ning when it leaps from high,
The vast bird swoops, with one long scream,
   Flung forward through the echoing sky.

But gallantly and cheerily
   The hunter shakes his faithful knife ;
Then with strung arm and measuring eye,
   Makes ready for the strife.

And for a moment, from between
   The covering wings of his wild foe,
His upturned face by all was seen,
   Untroubled wholly cheek and brow ;

But as the bold bird swept around,
 And keener shrill'd its frantic shriek,
At something in the savage sound,
 The hunter's heart grew weak.

Those gloomy wings above him spread,
 Cast, as he deemed, unnatural shade;
Whilst all about the eye-balls dread
 Unnatural heat and brightness played.

Bold as the sun, he yet had grown
 Among the grim and lonely hills,
Where many a legend dark, self-sown,
 The air with influence fills.

His solitary shepherd hours,
 In their wide silences were past,
Whilst gathering round him, viewless powers
 Their shadow on his spirit cast.

Weak only there, his nerves unstrung,
From early childhood ever drew
Omens from dreams, and blindly clung
To each wild tale that grew

On the night-covered mountain side,
Dim shapes which lurk away from men,
Under the hollow mists, that hide
The wailing stream, and haunted glen.

Hence in that breathless interim,
Ere the knife fell, like withering flame,
Each half-seen ghost and phantom grim
Across his memory came.

His strained sense imaged that it heard
The rocks with horrid laughter rife,
Whilst momently the demon-bird,
Grew larger into monstrous life.

Wild gibbering faces flickered near,
    Fantastic shapes convulsed the air,
A whisper glided round his ear,
    " It is a fiend—beware!"

Upwards he looked to the void heaven,
    And downwards on the dazzling main;
Whilst fiercely round and round were driven,
    The surges of his eddying brain.

He strikes at length, but on his eyes
    Danced giddily the white wave's gleam,
As the whirling rocks and the wavering skies,
    Rang to the eagle's scream.

There was dead silence upon high,
    And the tall forms of armèd men
Shone motionless against the sky,
    For a brief breathing-time, and then

Huge frames of giant height and bone
  Reeled all at once like foundering ships,
Whilst a low half-unconscious moan
  Slid from their quivering lips.

Not idly from his comrades true,
  Hissed forth that deep-drawn breath of
For the stout cord was severed through,
  To its last link of straining thread.

They fall together on their knees,
  With one short thrilling prayer for aid,
To the good saints who rule the seas,
  And the blest mother-maid.

Then without words their tasks they ply,
  Sick with alternate fear and hope;
Whilst the poor wretch instinctively

But still it holds together, still
   They lift him silently and slow,
Inch after inch with steady skill,
   Up from the depth below.

Hurrah! the arm of God can make
   Frail thread as firm as iron bands,
His power forbids it now to break,
   And safe the bloodless trembler stands.

The agony of that affright,
   One awful sign remained to show—
His hair went down as black as night,
   It rises white as snow.

THE MAMELUKE CHARGE.

Let the Arab courser go
Headlong on the silent foe;
Their plumes may shine like mountain snow,
Like fire their iron tubes may glow,
Their cannon death on death may throw,
Their pomp, their pride, their strength, we kn
But—let the Arab courser go.

The Arab horse is free and bold,
His blood is noble from of old,
Through dams, and sires, many a one,
Up to the steed of Solomon.

He needs no spur to rouse his ire,

His limbs of beauty never tire,'

Then, give the Arab horse the rein,

And their dark squares will close in vain.

Though loud the death-shot peal, and louder,

He will only neigh the prouder;

Though nigh the death-flash glare, and nigher,

He will face the storm of fire;

He will leap the mound of slain,

Only let him have the rein.

The Arab horse will not shrink back,

Though death confront him in his track;

The Arab horse will not shrink back,

And shall his rider's arm be slack?

No!—By the God who gave us life,

Our souls are ready for the strife.

We need no serried lines, to show

A gallant bearing to the foe.

We need no trumpet to awake

The thirst, which blood alone can slake.

What is it that can stop our course,

Free riders of the Arab horse?

Go—brave the desert wind of fire—

Go—beard the lightning's look of ire—

Drive back the ravening flames, which leap

In thunder from the mountain steep;

But dream not, men of fifes and drums,

To stop the Arab when he comes:

Not tides of fire, not walls of rock,

Could shield you from that earthquake shock.

Come, brethren, come, too long we stay,

The shades of night have rolled away,

Too fast the golden moments fleet,

Charge, ere another pulse has beat;

Before another breath is drawn,

Charge—like the tiger on the fawn.

LINES ON THE SALE OF THE BLACK ARAB,

THE GIFT OF THE IMAUN OF MUSCAT.

———

Yes! it is well that he should go,
  The matchless present of a king,
From ends so vile, and thoughts so low,
  As round the soul of England cling.

He was a horse for days of old,
  When British hearts were firm and true,
Unfit for times so mean and cold,
  And *that* the greedy pedlars knew;

They cared not, when to stranger-men
    The courteous monarch's gift was sent;
That link'd therewith, for ever then
    The honour of the people went.

They care not that the shameful tale
    Throughout the wavering East is borne,
Making the sellers, and the sale,
    A mark for just and hostile scorn.

What though with throbbing hearts we fear
    Strange terrors rushing from afar,
And daily rather feel than hear
    The stealthy tread of Russian war?

Great thoughts, great deeds, and feelings high,
    The sunshine of our British past,
All they can neither sell nor buy,
    To heaven or hell away they cast.

Yes ! it is well that he should go,

    The matchless present of a king,

From ends so vile, and thoughts so low,

    As round the soul of England cling.

The spirit of his Arab sires

    Would droop, as though in fetters bound,

With no reflection of its fires,

    From aught that moved or breathed around.

England of yore was full of men,

    Made strong to run a glorious course,

Of lion-port and eagle-ken,

    Fit riders for the Arab horse.

His high heart, then, like mingling flame,

    Into their brightness would have flowed ;

And, in his generous veins, the same

    Free spirit would have lived and glowed.

Such were the fearless few who stood
   Around a trembling tyrant's throne,
Eager to shed their dearest blood
   On freedom's primal altar-stone.

Such were the giants who upsprung
   Round her who crushed insulting Spain,
When, from our arms and hearts, we flung
   The fragments of the papal chain.

Such who, in old manorial halls,
   Which yet with loyal echoes ring,
Live still along the storied walls
   In armour for an outraged king.

Knights who at Naseby stood, and died
   Unbroken by the Roundhead boor,
Or from broad death-wounds swelled the tide
   Of faithful blood on Marston-moor.

But Faith, and Truth, and Chivalry,
   And emanating powers, have fled;
The veins of the worn earth are dry,
   By which each mighty growth was fed.

Scarce, through the gathering dimness, One
   True-hearted heir of ancient worth,
Shines, like the last ray of the sun,
   The night before the floods went forth.

The rest are shadows of an hour,
   A sapless, bloodless, boneless throng,
Without the spirit, or the power,
   For noble right, or strenuous wrong.

Amid the fog, and icy gloom,
   Round wither'd heart, and stunted brain,
We have not sympathy, or room
   For aught that shows a generous strain.

Then freely let the Arab go,
 That matchless present of a king,
From ends so vile, and thoughts so low,
 As round the soul of England cling.

WITH all his fearless chiefs around,

   The Moslem Ruler stood forlorn,

And heard at intervals, the sound

   Of drums athwart the desert borne.

To him a sign of fate, they told

   That Britain in her wrath was nigh,

And his great heart its powers unrolled

   In steadiness of will to die.

" Ye come, in your mechanic force,

 A soulless mass of strength and skill—

Ye come, resistless in your course,

 What matters it ?—'Tis but to kill.

A serpent in the bath, a gust

 Of venomed breezes through the door,

Have power to give us back to dust—

 Has all your giant empire more?

" Your thousand ships upon the sea,

 Your guns and bristling squares by land,

Are means of death—and so may be

 A dagger in a woman's hand.

Put forth the might you boast, and try

 If it can shake my seated will ;

By knowing when and how to die,

 I can escape, and scorn you still.

" The noble heart, as from a tower,
   Looks down on life that wears a stain ;
He lives too long, who lives an hour
   Beneath the clanking of a chain.
I breathe my spirit on my sword,
   I take my stand upon this stone,
And perish, to the last the Lord
   Of all that man can call his own."

Such was the mountain leader's speech ;
   Say ye, who tell the bloody tale,
When Havock smote the howling breach,
   Then did the noble savage quail?
No—when through dust, and steel, and flame,
   Hot steams of blood, and smothering smoke,
True as an arrow, to its aim
   The meteor-flag of England broke;

And volley after volley threw
A storm of ruin, crushing all,
Still cheering on a faithful few,
He would not *lose* his father's hall.
At his yet unpolluted door
He stood, a lion-hearted man,
And died, A FREEMAN STILL, before
The merchant thieves of **Frangistan**.

S O N G.

A FLOWER, a welcome flower, I bring
　　With drops of liquid diamond bright;
See, how the first moss-rose of spring,
　　Blooms for the ball to-night.

A fairy nursed the bud for you,
　　For you she warded off the blight;
And cherished it with heavenly dew,
　　For your first ball to-night.

Must of no magic laws make light,
Even when her beauty learns its power
Over the ball to-night.

Trusted by sylphs in fairy-land
  To bear their elfin-message right,
I claim to press that maiden-hand
  First at the ball to-night.

This is Titania's message, " Wear
  No other dress than simple white;
The rose alone in your bright hair,
  To charm the ball to-night.

" To other lovers use a tone
  Of civil but decided slight;
And on the bringer smile alone,
  At your first ball to-night."

TO A LADY

WHO WORE GREEN, THE COLOUR SACRED TO THE FAIRIES,

ON FRIDAY.

" I AM that lady of the air,
   The fairy Amabel :
I come from the rose-scented heart
   Of a distant Indian dell.
I have left the graceful jessamine,
   And flowers of burning bloom,
Whose cups are filled with fairy wine,
   To seek this wintry gloom.

" I was floating above my tuberose,
  (Deep-hearted queen of flowers,)
Drinking the fragrance of its love,
  In silent citron bowers;
I chased the bright-winged moths away,
  With passion's jealous care;
I folded it, from the sun's warm ray,
  And the embrace of air.

" Then I saw my page, that humming-bird
  Whom I dipped in a shooting star,
Burn through the green and quiet wood,
  Like a flying gem from far.
And he said, that a sullen English gnome,
  Who barbs the darts of snow,
From within his cold and lurid home,
  Had sworn to be thy foe.

" So I yoked my birds of Paradise,
  Whose speed knows no decay,
To a car of light, which I have framed
  Of the sun's violet ray.
And darted hither on the sigh
  Of a fairy-widowed rose ;
That the lightnings of mine eye
  Might chase away thy foes."

THE EPICUREAN.

How gently, beautiful and calm,
  The quiet river murmurs by,
How soft the light, how full of balm
  The breeze that soothes the dark'ning sk

In every clime, in every state,
  We may be happy if we will;
Man wrestles against iron fate,
  And then complains of pain and ill.

The flowers, the beasts, the very heaven,
   Calmly their destined paths pursue;
All take the pleasures that are given,
   We only, find them short and few.

Oh that mankind, alive to truth,
   Would cease a hopeless war to wage;
Would reap in youth, the joys of youth,—
   In age, the peacefulness of age.

Upon an everlasting tide
   Into the silent seas we go;
But verdure laughs along the side,
   And on the margin roses blow.

Nor life, nor death, nor aught they hold,
   Rate thou above their natural height;
Yet learn that all our eyes behold,
   Has value, if we mete it right.

Pluck then the flowers that line the stream,
　Instead of fighting with its power;
But pluck as flowers, not gems, nor deem
　That they will bloom beyond their hour.

Whate'er betides, from day to day,
　An even pulse, and spirit keep;
And like a child, worn out with play,
　When wearied with existence, sleep.

THE MANICHEAN.

How wonderful a place is earth!
　　To lend its gloom a single spark,
Birth must be death, and death be birth,
　　And even then, 'tis dark.

We know not whence, or how, we come,
　　We see not how, or where, we go;
And this, our only certain home,
　　It is a home of woe.

The mysteries that lie about,
 Warred on the fearless hearts of yore,
Till, in long combatings worn out,
 Their swords were keen no more ;

Unvexed, our fathers lived beneath
 The calming shadow of the cross;
How blest their power of simple faith !
 We can but mourn its loss :

That waning shadow will not cover
 Man's heart, as in its orient youth ;
Through its faint flutterings, we discover
 The wintry light of truth.

Far up as eye or thought can climb,
 We find the howling gale of life
Lashing the ancient floods of Time,
 From stillness into strife.

Swoops sudden, like a bird of prey,
  And tears the world in sunder;

Then light and love no more are seen,
  Death reigns, uncounterpoised by birth,
And a dense veil is drawn between
  The Lord of life, and earth :

Till the slow cycles roll it back,
  To its chill waking hour again,
Equipping it, to tread the track
  Of ancient doubt and pain.

Then time and space are loosed from high,
  Once more to shed deluding gleams
On a fresh pageant, peopled by
  Another crowd of dreams.

There are two powers, not made to die,
  Pursued and caught, and then pursuing,
Creation, everlastingly
  Alternating with Ruin.

Whether they wage an awful war,
  Or play a still more awful game,
Victims, or pawns, alike *we are*
  The sufferers in the same.

Happy who die, and are, as when
  These evil days had not begun;
But happier still as yet, the men
  Which have not seen the sun.

THE PLATONIST.

Father of Gods and men, on thee we call,
  Thou, who within the limits of thy soul,
Embracing all things, yet distinct from all,
  Spread'st life and order through the boundless whole.

It is the highest privilege of man,
  The crown, which philosophic virtue brings,
After long years of thought, aright to scan
  Thy presence, hidden under human things.

Not easy is the task—nor is it wise,
　　At large the holy secret to unfold;
Excessive light, into dim-seeing eyes,
　　Infuses darkness blinder than of old.

How noble are the Gods—that spring from thee,
　　The holy ones who made and bless us all—
Rivers of goodness, issuing from thy sea
　　Of Love, into whose deeps again they fall.

And we too are thy children, for within
　　Our dim and crowded hearts, under the strife
Of fleshly lusts, of passion, and of sin,
　　Burns on one spark of everlasting life.

A spark of heaven is given us, to keep clear
　　Of this foul dungeon's damp, that we may see,
A seed of heaven is set, for us to rear
　　Into a beautiful and deathless tree.

For this the toilsome circle was ordained,
   Lives new and multiform, unending still—
Until the soul its native seats has gained,
   Or sunk for ever to the gulfs of ill.

Turn not the spirit into flesh, nor grieve
   For virtue's sake to suffer and to die—
So after fewer transits, shalt thou leave
   Gross darkness, for a shining light on high.

THE cup of joy is found,
   A shallow draught and vain;
The cup of joy! but who shall sound
   The secret gulfs of pain?

The mystery of death—
   The mystery of birth—
The hourly groans that rise like breath
   From this bewildered earth,

Grow wild and wilder still
  In that expiring light,
Whose living lustre once could fill
  The ghastliness of night.

Alas! the star which poured
  Belief on pastoral men,
Through ages not in vain adored,
  Sets ne'er to rise agen.

And over earth is spread
  A grim rëentering gloom ;
Whilst doubts and fears contemned as dead
  Their ancient strength resume.

Sitting in sullen state
  Upon his joyless throne,
Daily becomes the sage's fate,
  More intimately known.

With all that heaven could shower
  Of gifts esteemed the best;
Health, wisdom, beauty, wealth and power,
  Only the unending rest

Of death seemed good to him;
  Yea better still to keep,
For ever in the regions dim
  Of ante-natal sleep;

But yet, however wise,
  Oh man! believe him not;
The noble realm of duty lies
  Within thy clouded lot.

Following her steady beam
  Across the waste abyss,
Taint not thy spirit with the dream
  Of future bale or bliss.

It well may be that God
　Sends immortality,
Earthwards from his unknown abode,
　To summon those who die.

And if when life is o'er
　Our fate is fixèd so,
Beyond the sable ocean's shore,
　We soon enough shall know.

Still let not hope debase,

THE CATHOLIC.

STILL, let not sordid hopes debase,
   Nor horrors over-awe,
Our love for her celestial face
   Whose name, is Truth and Law.

When, wooing vague and baseless d
   Man spurns all best control,
And drunken in his weakness, seem
   A God, to his own soul,

Oh! that the proud of heart could hear
   One sound of joyless mirth,
Could look upon the icy sneer
   Of him, who loves not earth.

" Duty," you say, " unto the wise,
   Blooms like a virgin bride,
With starry softness in her eyes,
   And Pleasure at her side."

Is Duty such?—Aye! who is then
   That mailed and sceptred queen,
Whose voice falls on the souls of men
   Consumingly serene?

" The Lifeblood of the Infinite,
   The Shadow of the Lord,
I am, to those who scan me right,
   A thing, and not a word.

" Did not my quenchless impulse fill
     The veins of the Most High,
The heart of God were numb and still,
     And the great world would die.

" Ye have stretched forth your arms, and striven
     As human strength may do,
There have been men who called on heaven—
     Which triumphed, they or you?

" The mighty men of old, have borne
     Burdens ye could not bear;
The warriors of the Cross, have worn
     Armour ye may not wear.

" The hands of *man* are sinewless
     To curb the tempted will,
Let him despair and die, unless
     God lift him upward still."

Low, but with spirit-withering might
   Glide in the words of power,
Darkening all courage, as a blight
   Dries up some joyous flower.

To our own purposes, we give
   At first unfearing trust,
By our own strength, we will to live,
   Holy, and wise, and just:

Till that calm scorn with pity blent,
   Breaks through the sleep of sin,
And our whole nature shudders, rent
   To its dim depths within.

Soul-smitten then, we writhe and pine
   In one unresting strife,
Seeking a promise, and a sign,
   Under the mask of life.

Till this wild world, around the brain,
    Reels like a feverish dream,
So that we know not in our pain
    Whether it be, or seem.

Is there no ray athwart the gloom?
    No hope for the distrest?
No one unwavering stay, on whom
    That weary world may rest?

Over Chaldean plains, a star
    Shed light and warmth on high,
Divine looks floated thence from far,
    As from a living eye,

A living eye, which showed to man
    A living God was there,
A Hope, a Promise, and a Plan,
    Not chaos and despair.

Until this withered heart of earth,
   So long a stagnant thing,
Rushed into blossom, like the birth
   Of bursting buds, in Spring.

Surely the elder years, no less
   Than this unquiet age,
Staggered in weight and weariness,
   Through their bleak pilgrimage.

Hunters of Wisdom, wasting Youth,
   And rest, and joy, and fame,
Have plunged into the gulphs of Truth,
   And Thought, till madness came :

And Bards have felt, beneath the curse,
   The heavens and earth grow black,
Questioning this veiled universe,
   Which gives no echo back.

And bitterer still, bereavèd love
   Has sorrowed on in vain,
No seraph answering from above,
   " Yet shall ye meet again."

There is no pang, no doubt, no dread,
   Thou idly striv'st to flee,
That slept not with the noble dead,
   Before it lived in thee;

The soul of man had dived, and soared,
   Through depths and heights sublime;
Plato had mused, and Homer poured
   His spirit upon Time,

Before the Lord of Calvary
   Under his thorny crown,
Looked in divine benignity
   Upon his murderers down.

Yet sages, weak with thought, which still
   Led to defeat and shame,
From their proud schools, to learn his will,
   As lisping children came,

And those, to whom this varied earth
   Was one sepulchral den,
Felt on their withered hearts, the birth
   Of Hope and life again.

No levity of jealous pride
   Fettered the deep assent;
Each eye unseal'd, at once descried
   What God and Nature meant.

They did not test each burning word
   By Logic's barren art,

Power touched their Spirits, as they knelt,
　　Like renovating dew,
God lived within them, and they felt,
　　Yea, *saw* that Christ was true.

Age teaching Age, flung forward light,
　　As out of beacon-pyres,
Till the rejoicing earth was bright
　　With countless mountain-fires.

The weak thence nerved, were strong to die
　　Exulting crowds before,
Calm, though the Lion's kindling eye
　　Glared through the grated door;

Full of meek hope, not only men,
　　But fragile girls, have seen
The slow unclosing of the den,
　　With nought but God between.

" Alas! that yonder spotless maid,
   So delicately fair,
Should through mean carnage, undismayed
   Be dragged, to perish there.

" Alas! for her, she stands alone,
   With large uplifted eye,
On the harsh sand, profusely thrown
   O'er planks it will not dry.

" No; not alas! she does not see
   The famished creature's rage,
There seems to her a company
   Of Angels round the cage.

" Aye, but if when the monster grim
   Rush roaring from his lair,
Over that awful interim,
   Lie only—vacant air,

" If that fresh flower, that lovely child,
    To the fanged savage cast,
By mocking fancies self-beguiled,
    Bleed for a dream, at last."

A dream—oh no, believe it not,
    Rather sink down, and die.
The Hope, that glorified her lot,
    Was deeper than a lie.

Have we another creed to make?
    Another God to raise,
Out of the Phantom forms, which shake
    These melancholy days?

Better to join the quiet dead,
    Than aimlessly live on,
With rayless heavens over-head,
    And faith for ever gone.

Let not the drunken pride of will
   In logic's glittering fence,
Entice thee to the ranks of ill,
   Against thy holier sense.

The Cross to save is as divine,
   The Spirit sword to quell,
As when of old, its primal sign
   Silenced unresting Hell.

Martyrs and saints, a reverent train,
   Gleams yet of glory cast;
Oh! sever not the golden chain
   That links thee to the past.

Pray with meek heart, and tearful eye,
   Fixing the inner mind
Upon that noble company,
   Who live in light behind.

Still to the man of humble knee,

    For human fear and grief,

The Church's old and mystic tree

    Has healing on its leaf.

THE CRUSADER'S RETURN.

(STANZAS FOR MUSIC.)

————— ——— —— · ——

At length we meet again, love—we meet, but where and
    how?
Dark time has rolled between us, but we stand together
    now;
The flowers I wreathed at parting, around thy sunny hair,
Have left nor sign nor shadow, of their blessèd presence
    there;

I have thought of thee, love, ever, through years of toil
    and pain;

Whilst the Syrian sun was burning down through thé very
    brain:

Whilst the dungeon damps were eating their way into my
    frame,

I have soothed my soul by dwelling on the music of thy
    name.

To thee the past is nothing, a dream of fled delight

Long gathered to its brothers, in the caverned gloom of
    night;

Through all the common channels thy life has glided by,

Whilst mine has been but one long wish, to see thee once
    —and die.

Rememberest thou the sunset, love, at the gleaming forest-
    well,

On thy young and blushing fondness how its mellowed
    radiance fell?

From an hour before its dawning, I had ridden fast and
    far,
To see thee in the spirit-light of the silver evening star;

Not the sand wind of the desert, in its swift and circling
    gloom,
Not the purple harbinger of the pitiless Simoom,
Not the dungeon roof of darkness, nor the howling storm
    of war,
Had power to stain that sunset—that silver evening star.

I blame thee not, belovèd—nay, I rejoice to see
How life and love conspire to breathe, their blessedness on
    thee;
I come in pain and sickness, like a leaf about to fall,
To look upon thy beauty, ere the spirit-voices call.

They call me, yes, belovèd, I hear them call me now;
Oh! joy unhoped, to perish with *thy* tears upon my brow;

Yet weep not for the wounded bird, who seeks that peaceful
    rest,
Where the wicked cease from troubling, and the weary are
    at rest.

THE SYRENS.

All the old tales of Evil Beauty in the Grecian Mythology are, I thir
tales of the sea, probably therefore of Phœnician origin; at any ra
the idea of Evil Beauty is not in accordance with the general charac'
of the Greek mind. I have endeavoured to obviate this anomaly,
making the Syrens the unwilling instruments of a destiny which th
can neither explain nor resist.

No rest—no pause—no change—Achnymene,
And thou, Phenusa, with thy shadowing hair
Thrown round the weepings of a heart outworn
To veil them from the sight—Belovèd ones,
Speak to me: is there any hope for us
But in ourselves? have we not inward strength

And sinews of the spirit, to control
This self-surrender to the powers of ill?

What though, like hovering clouds, about our home,
Slow moving ever to the moving sea,
Drift undulating ships—there—moss-grown rafts
The spoil of Caucasus, compact with oak,
And rough primeval pine trees interlaced;
Floating of old beneath gigantic forms
Who, urged by power malign, were hurried on
Down forest-shadowed rivers sounding wide,
To the great deep; thence under hostile stars
With rude art skirting this accursèd shore.
Here—tall Sidonian barks—Ægean boats
Built low for speed; and of the jealous isle
Full freighted argosies, for whose return
Even now the merchant kings are looking out
From the broad quays of Tyre—magnificent
With gold and pearl, and Tribute from afar.

What though the breath of our entrancing song

Heaps up, from age to age, around our feet

The mouldering bones of men, as the keen gales

Over Numidia, wide accumulate

Incessant hills of ever-heightening sand:

Still, oh belovèd sisters, not by us

Is the life drawn away out of the heart;

Not upon us, relentless Destinies,

The curse of the bereavèd rests—hour after hour,

Day after day, year after year, for ever,

Our prayers have wearied the vast halls of Heaven

That we might spare—but the Fates iron-nerved

Press close upon us, irremoveably,

And we but struggle, like a dragon writhing

Its hopeless folds under a stedfast rock.

Still, as the white sail from the distant sea

Uprises, slowly thickening into form

Above its peopled hull, our better nature

Glides from us like the shadow of a dream:

Still, the unbodied Demons with fierce glee,

And ravenous exactness, streaming up

From some unsounded depth of Acheron,

Pass into us, and shake the vacant soul

With Phantoms swarming from an evil will.

So that, instead of feeling gentle thoughts

And impulses of love, and happy hopes

Blossoming, one by one, like summer flowers,

As, in the days of old, when cherishing

A life, serenely passionless, yet soft,

We fed on beauty, beauty in all forms,

In all her aspects, ministrant on good.

Now fettered to some demon Lord unknown,

And doomed to execute his purposes,

We rush through horrible vicissitudes

Of stormy sin—passion—and pain—and chang

We shudder in an unimagined thirst

For human blood, in fits of hideous crime,

Alien desires, undreamt-of attributes,

And all the heat and darkness of deep Hell—

The sense of beauty, and the touch of good,

Till the foul mist dissolving, rushes out

In floods of sound, and headlong melodies,

Enriching the insatiate nets of death :

Whilst, ever pressing in upon the brain,

The air of heaven grows heated like a sea

Of fluctuating fires around, through which

Pale features and faint shapes are dimly seen,

Immoveably decaying, with bright eyes,

And indrawn breathings of husht ecstacy.

Until, the purpose being accomplishèd,

Back to his home the demon speeds, and we

Wildered, and weak, and panting, find ourselves

Among the silent faces of the dead, upon

The broadly blossoming shores of the full sea.

Say ! what avails it then, when we behold

The breathless aspect of the beautiful

Waning from beauty, or the loving heart

Shining unquenchable through dying eyes—

Say, what avails it, that we crowd the night

With moaning upon moaning, and repel

All thoughts of pleasure, and all hope of rest?

Girt, if we sleep, with ghastly multitudes,

Which wax and wane, and sever and combine,

And flit, and glare, and fade; as others still

Keep flickering up from the dim gulf of dreams,

To die past deaths again—gaunt mariners,

And bright-haired women, and the steel-clad strength

Of old sea-kings, with garments rich and strange,

And visages burnt in upon the brain—

So that our worn hearts, empty of delight,

Are wasted utterly, and drop away

In bitter weepings.—I have wept enough—

Year after year, in vague self-torturings,

I have stood nightly on moonlighted cliffs

Near the soft-sounding ocean—I have called

The everlasting stars to answer me

From their bright quietness; I have invoked

Forgotten names and forms of ancient Gods—

Ophion, and the mystic three who droop

From fading thrones, among the caverns old,

And on the clouded hills of Samothrace.

But not from these, nor from the younger heaven

Filled with rejoicing Gods, nor from beneath,

When, maddened with the sickness of suspense,

I have thrown loathing off, and called aloud

To the swart powers of sullen Erebus,

Down deepening through separate gulfs of death

Nor yet from that far God—the nameless one—

The everlasting—the unsearchable—

Who in his fathomless infinitude

Clasps equally the undivulged abyss

Of Darkness and the inmost home of Light,—

Has come or voice or token, to unfold

How we, of our own natures full of love,

As are the heavens of day, or the broad sea

Of waters,—in this solitary spot—

This desert isle—remote from Gods and men,

Can thus have earned, of the deaf universe,

Our weary and impenetrable doom.

Therefore, uplifting from my soul the load

Of the drear past—let the unanswering stars,

And the void air, and the unpitying heaven

Feel sorrow for the dead—*I* weep no more—

I will no longer yield my spirit up

To this—I will no longer be the slave

Of such forlorn and futile sympathies.

There is yet music sleeping in the lute,

Soft airs, and modulations, over which

There hangeth not the taint of human blood:

There are yet glories of the earth and sea,

And splendours in the sky—nor from the heart

Is absent the deep sense of solemn Joy,

Which rushes like a river, loosed from ice,

To greet the coming of the beautiful.

To them—to it—to all—to life and hope,

To poesy and nature, to the light
Of Loveliness, and the calm powers of J(
I dedicate myself.   There are yet ships
To moulder here, there are yet men to die
But what of that?   Death is the end of a
There are a thousand paths, a thousand g
On silent hinges ever opening in
To his black hall, so has it been decreed!
We are no more than one blind instrume
One, of the countless multitude, employe
To lead the shadowy sons of time and ch;
From heat and dust, from passion and fro
To their dim couches of unending rest.
We too shall die—in that unfathomed glo
There is a place for us, there is a home

Of something pleasurable sliding down
Throughout the blind abyss, as overhead
The earth renews itself unceasingly
In fruitage, and bright flowers, and everywhere
From her full breast of undecaying youth,
Life gushes into fountains of delight.

THE DREAM OF PILATE'S WIFE.

The same subject is much more successfully treated by my Friend Mr.
Milnes, in the Volumes which he has just published.

In the mild Eastern Spring-time, far away
    From Latian hills, and Tiber's yellow stream,
Upon a couch a Roman matron lay,
    And felt the awful presence of a dream :

To the blind sons of men, there was no more
    Than a fair woman sleeping through the night,
To rise to household duties as before,
    Or chase the fleeting shadow, called delight.

But Angels stood around in trembling love,
 Till the stern vision had unrolled its power,
And the whole chorus of the stars above
 Was hushed in humble silence at that hour.

What heart can number up the mystic throng
 Of shapes, down-drifting upon human eyes,
Through all the darkness that has flowed along,
 Since the first moonlight looked on Paradise?

There have been dreams of agonizing pain,—
 Of love—of bitter vengeance, of despair—
Of madness working in upon the brain,
 And wildly-woven trifles light as air:

Nor are they wanting to the fated few,
 By some fine sense, foreshadowing what will
Of deeper import, and of clearer hue,
 Than those thin phantoms which the million

But, whether bubble of the mind's emotion,
  Or prophet visions, over the grey foam
Of Time's unfathomed and unmeasured ocean,
  They pass in dim procession to their home;

Banded together in the twilight pale,
  Like shadows of a troop of ghosts, they weep
And flit about fantastically frail;
  Unwilling to go down into the deep;

But this was not as they : its task being done,
  With stately mien, and covered brow, it stood
Before that gibbering crowd, nor strove to shun,

And still within its nameless resting place

    The monarch of all dreams, upon its throne

It sits immoveably, with veilèd face,

    In unrevealing majesty—alone.

SAPPHO.

What power has caused the ocean swell,
   Like startled sleep, to flee?
What conquering Thessalian spell
   Breathed on the raging sea,
To sudden rest hath bowed and bent
The soul of the wild element?

Nothing is there, save one sweet bird,
　　Yet as she glideth on,
With wing that moves through heaven unheard,
　　Wave after wave is won,
Under her shadow soft to lie
Lulled into clear tranquillity.

It is the halcyon, holy thing!
　　To whom the gods have given;
That the sea should smile beneath her wing,
　　And reflect the bright blue heaven
Unsullied, and serenely fair,
As the dreams of my youthful spirit were.

The halcyon flitteth to and fro,
　　Above the charmèd sea;
My thoughts like troubled waters flow,
　　Why comes she not to me?
Why calms she not the waves of pain,
Which vex this weary heart and brain?

My harp is silent at my side,
  It has been silent long;
Vainly these trembling hands have tried
  To wake it into song.
My soul is full of one desire—
One dream—one fever-fit—one fire.

At every sound mine ears have caught,
  This heart has throbbed so fast,
That broken down, and over-wrought
  It hardly beats at last;
Ebbing from hot and bitter strife,
To utter weariness of life.

My cheek is wan—my pulse is low,
  With waiting here alone;
I cannot stay, I cannot go.
  Oh! that the day were done;
Oh! that some power my brain would steep
  In slumber motionless and deep.

Oh bear me to some forest glade,

   Far from this glaring sun,

Where, dark with overhanging shade,

   The fresh cold waters run;

If God and nature fail to cure,

The hand of healing death is sure.

TARPEIA.

In yonder magic hill,
   There is a dungeon deep,
Wherein, girt round with darkness, still
   Tarpeia sits, in sleep.

Let no rude murmur break
   The charmèd trance of sin;
It were not good, for man to wake
   The maid, who sleeps within.

For many an age, she sate,
   Forbid to rest or die;
Fast fettered by the hand of fate
   To quenchless agony.

Wreathed flames around her head
   Were fastened by a spell;
The gems, upon her neck, were fed
   With lurid light from hell.

And as the inmost hill
   Shook to her speechless pain;
Insulting demon-voices still
   Kept singing on their strain.

That is the crown of gold
   Which made this rock your home;
Those are the jewels, for which you sold
   The warlike sons of Rome.

Such was Tarpeia's doom,
    Within the grim hill side;
Until that day of mystic gloom,
    When God for sinners died.

Since that, these pangs no more
    Her heavy slumbers chase;
God grant, that by the penance sore,
    Her soul may have found grace.

Still, let no murmurs break
    The charmèd trance of sin;
It were not good, for man to wake
    The maid who sleeps within.

THE HYPERBOREAN MAIDEN.

"These Hyperborean virgins died in Delos . . . . Their sepulchre is on the e t hand, within a spot consecrated to Diana, and covered by an olive-tree."

HERODOTUS.

SCYTHIAN.

WHAT does this olive here?

DELIAN PRIEST.

Its branches weave a holy gloom,

Over the northern maiden's tomb,

Throughout the year:

She came from a land that is far away,

Where the brightness of our southern day

Is all unknown,

To listen to our Delian god;

And here, beneath the flowery sod,

    She sleeps alone.

And this olive rose up silently,

To shade with its sacred canopy,

    Her quiet sleep :

And our Delian virgins every year,

With solemn music come, and here

    Bend down to weep;

Whilst all the flowers of Greece are shed

Above the Scythian damsel's head.

SCYTHIAN.

It is not beneath the olive shade,

That a northern maiden should be laid,

    Deep though it be,

Nor within these marble halls of pride;

    Her spirit free

Should dwell, where the cool breeze at even

Brings whispers of her native heaven.

And your God should have called a stately tree,

From the forests that frown o'er the northern sea,

　　　Her tomb to shade:

　　　He should have called a mighty pine,

　　　With gnarlèd boughs, and knotted rind,

　　　To catch the roarings of the wind,

　　　Where she is laid:

For the olive, and the purple vine,

Though bright in the sun their green leaves shine,

　　　Know not the maid;

But the solemn tree of the north, would spread

Its shadow in love o'er her narrow bed;

And the breath of the simple flowers that blow

At the melting of the northern snow,

Would lend delight to the visions of death,

When she dreameth silently beneath.

THE ATHENIAN PŒAN AT MARA⌐

The beginning and end of this composition, are to be
inherited battle hymn of the Ionian race; of that branch (
which was seated in Attica. In the middle I have adde⌐
pointing to the particular emergency; there was, I apprel
addition in point of fact; but I think myself justified
supposing it to have been made, considering the terror of t
and the unusual importance of the crisis.

OnCE more, a threatening trumpet

Across our skies is borne;

Once more, a foeman's footstep

Tramples Ionian corn.

In thy stern Father's shining hall,
  Pallas Athene hear,
Be thou to us a brazen wall,
  Be thou our shield and spear;
Ionian Goddess undefiled,
Unmothered and unwedded child
  Of the Eternal name,
When we call upon thee, hear us,
In the mist of strife be near us,
Be a strong arm, to uprear us
  From the gulphs of death and shame;
Be a keen unwaning star,
With threatening might
Of arrowy light,
Piercing the cloud of hostile war.
With them are Alien Gods—be *thou*
Among us, and about us, now.

Down from thy Father's shining halls,
  With meteor swiftness leap,

That baleful trumpet-note which passed,

  Was waked by no Hellenic lips,

Those shadows on yon sea, are cast,

  Not from Corinthian ships.

Not now—along the river bank

  Careering wild and wide,

With lances set against our flank,

  Thessalian horsemen ride.

No Thracian drives his battle car

From black Pangæan heights afar,

  Nor swelleth loud a Theban shout,

  Nor Isle of Pelops poureth out

    Her floods of Dorian war;

But hither from wild homes are rolled,

  The grim clans of the restless Mede,

Men, whom untravelled regions breed,

  And Gods unknown uphold;

In yonder shining files have place

The Syrians of the iron mace,

The Lords of the Cilician steed,

The Bactrian, with his bow of reed,

  The Paricanian spear,

The Arab shafts that never fail,

The scales of Persia's glittering mail,

  And Libyan cars of fear.

Yet, though the Median Lord be great,

Wanton in wealth, and drunk with hate,

Others, as mighty in estate,

Have fallen into cureless ill:

Yes, though the Median Lord be great,

  Greater and mightier still,

Are those, who pass through heaven's high gate,

  To work their father's will;

Therefore, in calmness we await
This travail of incumbent fate,
Because we know that thou can'st smite
His myriads into instant flight.

Now, ye shouts of men go round,
Now, ye quickening trumpets sound,
Now, each fife and clarion
Fling the battle-music on,
Fling forward, as a gathering flood,
The ancient melody of blood :
Like a beacon, let it dart
From lip to lip, from heart to heart,
    For great Athene hears,
From rank to rank, from line to line,
She glides a spirit and a sign,
    Up with the old Ionian spears :
Hark ! how her haughty footstep treads
Like living thunder o'er our heads,

Mark! where through æther's mystic veil
Burn glimpses of her gleaming mail;
The brazen shield is darkening o'er us,
The brazen lance is bright before us,
Ionian Goddess! Maid divine,
We follow, where they move and shine.

DIDO'S ANSWER TO ÆNEAS IN

These versés are founded on the dreary Homeric
staté, according to which nothing but mere being rem

The chill blue lake of Acheron,

    Whose flood has never moved at all;

The dim grey forest, overgrown

    With withered leaves which do not fall;

The still mist seated on the herbless ground;

The numb sky, barren of all light and sound;

These are not merely dreams, the spawn

    Of Chaos and unmeaning Fate,

But pictured types around us drawn

    To image forth Man's inward state,

As soon as Time, ebbing in giant waves,

Has rolled him down through Death's unsounded caves

The earth, the air, the sea, the sky,

    Lovely in unrelaxing change,

With deepest harmonies reply

    To Life in all her boundless range:

Even so accords, this wan unmoving gloom,

With what our spirits are beyond the tomb.

You ask me to forgive—'Tis vain,—

  We have not here the human will;

Nor feelings now, nor powers remain

  To wish thee either good or ill :

The shapes that sail around care not for thee;

I am the same with them, and they with me.

Once bound for this unchanging place,

  One solemn change all undergo;

Though still ourselves, we lose all trace

  Of that which used to make us so :

One vast and shadowy soul, diffused in each,

Gives us our phantom thought and dreaming speech.

FROM THE GREEK.

Alas! the mallows, when along the dale
They fade and perish—when the parsley pale
And the bright-leaved anethus droops—once more
These live, and bloom in beauty, as before.
But we—the wise, the warlike, and the great,
Wither beneath the touch of death—and straight
Sleep, deaf within the hollow earth, a sleep
For ever lengthening, limitless, and deep.

SONNET.

Thus sung the ancient bark of Sicily,
   The shepherd poet—as he wandered forth,
And saw the flowers of summer droop and die,
   Under the touch of the malignant north,

What charms, and magic drugs, conspired to steep

The poet's heart in darkness and despair?

How dull a thought! that God, whose love can bless

The falling rose, and tend the worm with care,

Made man a living soul—for nothingness.

THE DAUGHTER OF HIPPIAS.

FROM SIMONIDES.

———

THIS turf lies on a woman's breast,
Shrouded in deep and peaceful rest;
The seion of a royal tree,
Mother, and wife of kings, was she;
Yet, though to these high names allied,
Her gentle spirit knew not pride.

SONNET.

Her father was a man of violent mood,
   Hated—and hating many.—Restless fear
Alternately, and burning anger glowed
   Beneath his heart—and death seemed ever near,

Such multitudes were thirsting for his blood.

But she was young, and beautiful, and mild

As is the morning star—in their own clime,

Taught by her natural love, though yet a child,

She sung to him, and smiled his cares away :

Thus did she ever in her maiden prime,

And when his head in foreign lands was grey,

She soothed him still with love that grew not dull,

And stood before him, striving to be gay,

With pleading eyes, divinely beautiful!

LEAF-TINTED through the vines, a ray of green
Is playing from the horizontal sun,
And fast, beneath yon plane-tree's deepening screen,
The fresh cold waters darken as they run ;
And there, an old man of majestic mien,
Sitting with silver hair, and eye serene,
Muses on Time and on Eternity—
On the bold hopes, in which his youth begun,
The much accomplished, the more left undone :
Draw near with reverence, for this is he
Who heard the eyeless father's cursings wild
Fall on the hostile twins, who called up thee,
High-soul'd Electra, and that orphan child
Antigone, as lofty, and more mild :

CONTINUED.

Upon the setting sun he gazed, whose light

An emblem of himself, before him lay,

Poised in mild beauty on the edge of night,

The dreams that dazzled morning with delight,

The splendours of hot noon, had passed away,

And Repose came before the tomb, a sight

Serenely sacred in its calm decay ;

For as life faded, underneath the sway

Of an immortal spirit, evermore

Brighter and keener like a kindling star,

Dilating inwardly, the frantic jar

Of struggling lusts, and passions deemed before

Resistless, now became submiss and still,

No more enchaining the distorted will.

CONTINUED.

And men came round him, eager to drink in

Of the freed spirit's everlasting day.

But one there was, whom shame could not reprove,

Nor holy age abash—nor wisdom win

To put aside the thoughts of earth and sin.

"Tell me," he cried, "can woman's quickening eye

Still thaw thee into transient youth, and move

Thy frozen blood from its thin apathy;

Or is the sense of pleasure dead within?"

Thus spoke he, either of a scornful mind,

Or to all moral beauty, deaf and blind.

CONTINUED.

As if an eagle, whose unfaltering flight

Sweeps through the halls of sunshine, with a range

Wide as the sky, should plunge into a night

Of freezing clouds, before they reached his sight:

Thus, with a sudden sense of painful change,

As into stormy darkness out of light

The hearers passed—heaven-taught by hopes sublime.

The Poet answered, "Thou art yet enthralled

In the foul webs of sense be wise in time:

The privilege of age, is to be called
Out of life's whitening ashes, to a clime
And region of calm thought, a glorious realm,
Where Truth and Freedom reign, divine exchange
For passions which enslave and overwhelm."

CONCLUDED.

Ay ! even then, when health and strength sunk low
When each temptation to indulge desire
Crumbled away upon life's failing fire,
And Earth, with all her gifts, arose to go ;
Happy, if even then the soul might shew
Some shadow of her origin divine,
And with fresh hopes, and zeal renewed, aspire
To wrestle with her maimed and wearied foe.
Mean though we be, our state through Christ is hig
A Power flows to us from his awful sign,
Which is both spear and shield, wherewith to face
And conquer, though in baleful powers arrayed,
Those unseen kings, to whom man's hapless race
Homage of old inevitable, paid.

THEN with stern looks in answer spoke,
  Achilles famed for speed;
" Oh wretch in insolence attired!
  Oh spirit bent on greed!
Why should the Greeks thy words obey?
  Why should they journeys take?
And stoutly, against warlike men,
  Do battle for thy sake?

" Not through the spear-armed sons of Troy,
  Came I to fight and slay;
They wronged not me, they drove no steer,
  No steed of mine away;

In the fertile fields of Phthia
    They spoiled no fruits, I ween,
For many are the shadowy cliffs,
    And loud the sea between.

" Abandoned wretch ! we followed thee,
    We came to please thy heart ;
Honouring thy brother, and thyself,
    All shameless as thou art :
Yet though we only came to Troy
    In answer to that call,
Ye never waste a thought on us,
    Or care for us at all.

" Nay more, thou threatenest me, that thou,
    Thyself wilt seize my spoil,
That which the children of the Greeks
    Gave after all my toil :
And yet my prize ne'er equals thine,
    Whenc'er the Greeks destroy,

And plunder of the wealth it holds,
  Some peopled town of Troy.

" The burden of the raging war
  Falls on these hands of mine;
But when the time of sharing comes,
  Far larger gifts are thine :
And I retire to my ships,
  When wearied in the fight,
With some trifle, which I love, because
  It is my own by right.

" But now to Phthia I return,
  'Tis the best course for me,
Once more, with all my curvèd ships,
  To cross the sounding sea:
No longer stay I here, when thus
  Dishonoured by thyself,
That *thou* mayest fatten on the spoil
  And drain the land of pelf."

“ Lead forth my gallant myrmidons
 The battle shock to meet,
For the dark cloud of Trojan war
 Hangs grimly o'er our fleet:
The Argive troops are fettered in
 Along the ocean strand,
Scantly maintaining as their own,
 That narrow strip of land:
But the whole of Troy is rushing on,
 Without a thought of fear;
No longer see they now the front
 Of *my* helmet blazing near.

Had the king's words to me been mild,

    How soon they would have fled,

And left the trenches in our camp

    Filled to the brim with dead :

Now, though they hem our army round,

    No Diomed is near;

Not in his hands, to save and guard,

    Flashes the ravening spear.

From the hated head of Agamemnon,

    I hear no shouts resound ;

But those of the man-quelling Hector

    Are bursting loud around;

He calls his Trojans on, and they

    With a cry of wild delight

Cover the whole of the wide plain,

    Conquering the Greeks in fight."

ODYSSEY.

Book XX. line 345.

She kindled fits of frantic mirth,

   Maddening their hearts the while,

But suddenly their laughter sunk

   To a convulsive smile :

The flesh they eat grew foul with gore,

   Strange tears began to flow,

And something in the secret soul

   Prompted their hearts to woe :

Then outspake Theoclymenus,

   (These were the words he said,)

" What evil doom, O wretched men,

   Vexes you now ?   Each head,

Each face, down to the knees below,

    Is swathed in darkness dread.

Low wailing murmurs spread like fire,

    Tears down your cheeks have flowed,

The walls, and all the lintels round,

    Are dabbled o'er with blood;

Yon porch is full of shadowy forms,

    Full too this stately room,

Together gliding duskily

    Down into Stygian gloom;

And over all the place beneath,

    A deadly mist hath run;

And some one, from the heaven above,

    Has blotted out the sun."

He ceased—On this, right merrily

    They all to laugh begun.

THE END.

LONDON:

BLATCH AND LAMPERT, PRINTERS, GROVE PLACE, BROMPTON.